W9-CFH-451

ANTHROPOSOPHY
IN EVERYDAY LIFE

ANTHROPOSOPHY
IN EVERYDAY LIFE

Rudolf Steiner

ANTHROPOSOPHIC PRESS

This edition copyright © 1995 by Anthroposophic Press.

Published by Anthroposophic Press
P.O. Box 749, Gt. Barrington, MA 01230
www.steinerbooks.org

"Practical Training in Thought" [Praktische Ausbildung des Denkens] was given by Rudolf Steiner in Karlsruhe, January 18, 1909, and is included in *Die Beantwortung von Welt- und Lebensfragen durch Anthroposophie* (volume 108 of the Bibliographic Survey, 1986). Copyright © 1966 by Anthroposophic Press.

"Overcoming Nervousness" [Nervosität und Ichheit] was given in Munich, January 11, 1912, and is included in *Erfahrungen des Übersinnlichen Die Wege der Seele zu Christus* (volume 143 of the Bibliographic Survey, 1961). It was translated from the German original by R. M. Querido and Gilbert Church. Copyright © 1969 by Anthroposophic Press, Inc. It was retranslated by Michael Lipson for this edition. Copyright © 1995 by Anthroposophic Press.

"Facing Karma" [Grundstimmung dem Menschlichen Karma gegenuber] was given in Vienna, February 8, 1912, and is included in *Das esoterische Christentum* (volume 130 in the Bibliographic Survey, 1961). It was translated from the original by Dietrich V. Asten. Copyright © 1975 by Anthroposophic Press, Inc.

"The Four Temperaments" [Das Geheimnis der menschlichen Temperamente] was given in Berlin, March 4, 1909, and is included in *Wo und wie findet man den Geist?* (volume 57 in the Bibliographic Survey, 1984). It was translated from the German by Brian Kelly. Copyright © 1987 by Anthroposophic Press, Inc.

ISBN 0-88010-427-9

Library of Congress Cataloging-in-Publication Data is available.

Seventh printing, 2007

Printed in the United States of America by McNaughton & Gunn, Inc.

Contents

Introduction

A major task facing humanity as it moves into the new millennium is that of uniting spiritual and practical life.

In the Middle Ages—the time of Christendom—science, art, religion, and society were still to a great extent united. Untold monks and nuns labored and loved mightily for the sake of God and the world. Their lives of prayer and devotion, centered around the Eucharist, kept the interior flame of worship burning brightly. Radiating outward, the spiritual consequences of their steadfastness resonated throughout the landscape, impregnating villages, towns, and cities with a sense of the divine presence in the world.

At this time, too, great Cathedrals and humble churches alike filled ordinary people with the understanding that every aspect of life participated in God's purpose. Scholars, philosophers, scientists, and crafts people—all of whom contributed to the creation of a sacramental vision of the world in which each thing and every human act were imbued with spiritual significance—gathered around these Houses of the Spirit, amplifying its effectiveness.

This pervasive sense of the sacred also existed in earlier, pre-Christian times, when the priests and hierophants of the ancient Mystery Centers and Temples coordinated human culture in a way that permitted the spirit to realize itself in the manner appropriate to the moment. But, with the rise of the Modern Age, a powerful cleft was driven between human beings, nature, and the divine. We may call the process "secularization." Religion and spiritual life became increasingly marginalized. Instead of spiritual realities, human beings pursued this-worldly ends, such as comfort and wealth. Thus, gradually, the thread connecting saints and esoteric masters with the general life of humanity was broken; meaning fragmented; and the sacramental relation of human beings to each other and the cosmos ceased to function. Materialism in its many guises—positivism, Darwinism, Marxism etc.—now became the guiding principle in science and society. Religion and culture—religion and the state—were separated and spiritual, religious life became a question of individual responsibility.

This was a heavy burden to bear for individuals who had not only to create a spiritual life for themselves, but increasingly had to do so in opposition to the very quarters from which help might have been expected. For, as society plunged into materialism, the Churches, not wishing to be left out, joined willingly in the descent. There were, of course, exceptions to this tendency, but such generally was the situation at the beginning of the twentieth century when Rudolf Steiner (1861–1925) began to teach, initially under the auspices of the Theosophical Society.

As a natural clairvoyant, of great spiritual gifts, Steiner began his journey by assimilating the best of what the culture of his time had to offer. He chose for himself a scientific-technical education. At the same time, realizing the need to transform our present consciousness so that it might become a vehicle of spiritual knowledge, he undertook a phenomenological study of the processes by which we come to know—what is called "epistemology." Up against the pervasive influence of the philosopher Kant, who maintained that we could never truly know anything in itself but only our own forms of thought, Steiner knew from his own experience as a free spiritual being that the possibility of brain-free thinking lay within the capacity of human beings who thus could know truly and fully the world's actual spiritual reality. In two central early works—*Truth and Knowledge* and *Intuitive Thinking as a Spiritual Path*[1]—he laid the ground for what he would accomplish in the future. He was greatly helped in this work of preparation by prolonged study and meditation on the scientific works of Goethe, which he was asked to edit for a new edition of the Complete Works—the Kürschner "*Deutschen Nationalliteratur*" edition. From this, too, a series of fundamental, ground-breaking texts resulted.[2]

During this period, though already initiated into his spiritual task, Steiner was still very much a free thinker of his time.[3] Then, as he wrote in his *Autobiography*, "shortly before the turn of the century," a profound experience was given to him: an experience that "culminated in my standing in the spiritual presence of the Mystery of Golgotha in a most profound and solemn festival of knowledge."[4] This experience marked a call. Shortly thereafter, he left the literary and philosophical world of letters and joined his destiny to the movement for the renewal of spiritual knowledge in our time.

The tasks lying before him were manifold. In order to undertake them, he realized that, acting wholly and freely out of the spirit, he would also have to connect himself horizontally with

1. Both are available from Anthroposophic Press.
2. See the following works of Rudolf Steiner published by Mercury Press, Spring Valley, New York (also available from Anthroposophic Press): *Goethean Science*; *Goethe's World View*; *The Science of Knowing*.
3. See, for instance, Rudolf Steiner, *Friedrich Nietzsche, Fighter for Freedom* and *Individualism in Philosophy*.
4. Steiner, *An Autobiography* (Blauvelt, New York: Steinerbooks, 1991) p. 319.

the various traditions flowing together to herald the possibility of a "new age of light."[5]

He linked himself first to the Theosophical Society founded by H. P. Blavatsky, becoming the Secretary of the German Section. From the very beginning, he made complete independence and autonomy the condition of his taking on this task. Thus, as an independent spiritual teacher, working within the Theosophical Society, Steiner began to lecture freely from his own experience on spiritual matters. At the same time, he began to work more esoterically—transforming the legacy of masonic, hermetic, and esoteric Christian streams and taking on esoteric students. From this period (1904–1910) date what would become the basic texts of Anthroposophy.[6] But Anthroposophy itself, under that name, would not arise as a separate, independent spiritual movement until 1913 when, as a result of the controversy surrounding the young Krishnamurti—whether he was, or was not, the reincarnation of Christ—Steiner split permanently from the Adyar theosophists.[7]

From the beginning, Steiner saw his task as the rescue of humanity from materialism and secularism. He knew that for evolution—the divine work of the Gods—to continue in an organic, healthy direction, the world and human beings— which are essentially not two, but one—must once again be

---

5. According to Rudolf Steiner the Kali Yuga—or Dark Age—ended in 1899, opening the way to a new age of light.
6. The so-called "Basic Books" of Rudolf Steiner are: *Intuitive Thinking as a Spiritual Path: A Philosophy of Freedom; Christianity as Mystical Fact; How to Know Higher Worlds, Theosophy*; and *Occult Science, An Outline.*
7. The Anthroposophical Society was founded on February 3, 1913. It was refounded as The General Anthroposophical Society, with Rudolf Steiner as its President, on New Year 1923/4. See Rudolf Steiner, *The Christmas Conference* (Hudson, New York: Anthroposophic Press, 1989).

seen and lived as the profound spiritual reality they are. The task of Anthroposophy, he recognized, could not proceed piecemeal, but called for a renewal of culture as a whole—a bringing together of science, religion, and art in a sacred unity. It was in this sense that Steiner described the work of Anthroposophy as the renewal of the ancient Mysteries. But renewal here does not mean repetition. The old must die away for the new to come into being. But it cannot simply be replaced by something already known, no matter how illustrious or well tested. Rather, something new must be created. But such a new revelation can no longer be received passively from the Gods, as was the case in previous epochs. It must now be created by, in, and through human beings.

This clearly is a great work. Yet this critical, cosmically important undertaking begins in the simplest, humblest ways, as the four lectures included in the collection show. After all, if it is upon human beings that the task of evolution depends, then there is no choice but to begin with human beings as they are. We must begin with ourselves, where we are: with our ordinary daily selves.

Therefore, though it is often thought that spiritual paths like Anthroposophy bear no connection to practical life, this is a profound misconception. Practical life is indubitably the beginning of the way—as, in a certain sense, it is also the end. After all, the work of evolution is practical work—in and on the world. Besides this, as these lectures demonstrate, working out of a spiritual perspective can enhance our ability to deal creatively with the varied situations destiny brings us in life, while at the same time opening us to the presence of spiritual realities in our daily life.

The first lecture, "Practical Training in Thought," concerns the fundamental human activity of *thinking*. All we do, we do through thinking. Often, however, we discount this fact as "mere thinking." First, then, we must realize the suprapersonal, transcendent *reality* of thinking, and that thinking is related to the "I" or higher self.

The second lecture, "Overcoming Nervousness," shows how further exercises in thinking that work toward strengthening the everyday I—while pointing the way to the higher I—also provide the calm center necessary to lead purposeful, healthy lives.

The third lecture, "Facing Karma," takes us to the heart of life, to the place where we experience suffering and happiness. How are we to understand *spiritually* the various trials and tribulations life brings us? Understanding the law of karma— that determines whom and what we encounter—helps us to develop self-knowledge in a larger sense. By this we are enabled to transform and attune ourselves to the larger psycho-spiritual cosmos of which we are a part.

Finally, in "The Four Temperaments," we learn how the union of hereditary factors and our own inner spiritual natures shapes our psychology: who we are. The guide here is the ancient tradition of the four temperaments—sanguine, choleric, phlegmatic, and melancholic—the renewed understanding of which allows us to develop a truly modern spiritual psychology that must be the basis of any true self knowledge.

In the past, the lectures in this collection have been available only in booklet form. As such, they were among the best loved and most used in the anthroposophical canon. It is our hope that, in this new form, they will find new and more abundant life—new readers, new walkers on the path of the respiritualization of human life on earth.

Christopher Bamford

Practical Training in Thought

Karlsruhe, January 18, 1909

It may seem strange that an anthroposophist should feel called upon to speak about practical training in thought, for there is a widespread opinion that anthroposophy is highly impractical and has no connection with life. This view can only arise among those who see things superficially, for in reality what we are concerned with here can guide us in the most ordinary affairs of everyday life. It is something that can be transformed at any moment into sensation and feeling, enabling us to meet life with assurance and to acquire a firm position in it.

Many people who call themselves practical imagine that their actions are guided by the most practical principles. But if we inquire more closely, we find that their so-called "practical thought" is often not thought at all but only the continuing pursuit of traditional opinions and habits. An entirely objective observation of the "practical" person's thought and an examination of what is usually termed "practical thinking" will reveal the fact that it generally contains little that can be called practical. What to them is known as practical thought or thinking consists in following the example of some authority whose ideas are accepted as a standard in the construction of some object. Anyone who thinks differently is considered impractical because this thought does not coincide with traditional ideas.

When something really practical has been invented, it has often been done by a person without practical knowledge of that particular subject. Take, for instance, the modern postage stamp. It would be most natural to assume that it was invented by some practical post office official. It was not. At the beginning of the last century it was a complicated affair to mail a letter. In order to dispatch a letter one had to go to the nearest receiving office where various books had to be referred to and many other formalities complied with. The uniform rate of postage known today is hardly sixty years old, and our present postage stamp that makes this possible was not invented by a practical postal employee at all but by someone completely outside the post office. This was the Englishman, Rowland Hill.

After the uniform system of postage stamps had been devised, the English minister who then had charge of the mails declared in Parliament that one could not assume any simplification of the system would increase the volume of mail as the impractical Hill anticipated. Even if it did, the London post office would be entirely inadequate to handle the increased volume. It never occurred to this highly "practical" individual that the post office must be fitted to the amount of business, not the business to the size of the post office. Indeed, in the shortest possible time this idea, which an "impractical" man had to defend against a "practical" authority, became a fact. Today, stamps are used everywhere as a matter of course for sending letters.

It was similar with the railroads. When in 1837 the first railroad in Germany was to be built, the members of the Bavarian College of Medicine were consulted on the advisability of the project and they voiced the opinion that it would be unwise to build railroads. They added that if this project were to be carried out, then at least a high board fence would have to be erected on both sides of the line to protect the public from possible brain and nervous shock.

When the railroad from Potsdam to Berlin was planned, Postmaster General Stengler said, "I am now dispatching two stagecoaches daily to Potsdam and these are never full. If people are determined to throw their money out the window, they can do it much more simply without building a railroad!"

But the real facts of life often sweep aside the "practical," that is to say, those who believe in their own ability to be practical. We must clearly distinguish between genuine thinking and so-called "practical thinking" that is merely reasoning in traditional ruts of thought.

As a starting point to our consideration I will tell you of an experience I had during my student days. A young colleague once came to me glowing with the joy of one who has just hit upon a really clever idea, and announced that he must go at once to see Professor X (who at the time taught machine construction at the University) for he had just made a great discovery. "I have discovered," he said, "how, with a small amount of steam power and by simply rearranging the machinery, an enormous amount of work can be done by one machine." He was in such a rush to see the professor that that was all he could tell me. He failed to find him, however, so he returned and explained the whole matter to me. It all smacked of perpetual motion, but after all, why shouldn't even that be possible? After I had listened to his explanation I had to tell him that although his plan undoubtedly appeared to be cleverly thought out, it was a case that might be compared in practice with that of a person who, on boarding a railway car, pushes with all his might and then believes when it moves that he has actually started it. "That," I said to him, "is the thought principle underlying your discovery." Finally, he saw it himself and did not return to the professor.

It is thus quite possible to shut ourselves up within a shell fashioned by our own thoughts. In rare cases this can be observed distinctly, but there are many similar examples in life that do not always reach such a striking extreme as the one just cited. Someone who is able to study human nature more intimately, however, knows that a large number of thought processes are of this kind and often sees, we might say, people standing in the car pushing it from within and believing that they are making it move. Many of the events of life would take a different course if people did not so often try to solve their problems by thus deluding themselves.

True practice in thinking presupposes a right attitude and a proper feeling for thinking. How can a right attitude toward thinking be attained? Anyone who believes that thought is merely an activity that takes place within the head or the soul cannot have the right feeling for thought. Whoever harbors this idea will be constantly diverted by a false feeling from seeking right habits of thought and from making the necessary demands on thinking. A person who would acquire the right feeling for thought must say, "If I

can formulate thoughts about things, and learn to understand them through thinking, then these things themselves
must first have contained these thoughts. The things must
have been built up according to these thoughts, and only
because this is so can I in turn extract these thoughts from
the things."

It can be imagined that this world outside and around us
may be regarded in the same way as a watch. The compari-
son between the human organism and a watch is often
used, but those who make it frequently forget the most
important point. They forget the watchmaker. The fact
must be kept clearly in mind that the wheels have not
united and fitted themselves together of their own accord
and thus made the watch "go," but that first there was the
watchmaker who put the different parts of the watch
together. The watchmaker must never be forgotten.
Through thoughts the watch has come into existence. The
thoughts have flowed, as it were, into the watch, into the
thing.

The works and phenomena of nature must be viewed in
a similar way. In the works of human beings it is easy to
picture this to ourselves, but with the works of nature it is
not so easily done. Yet these, too, are the result of spiritual
activities and behind them are spiritual beings. Thus, when
a person thinks about things he or she only re-thinks what
is already in them. The belief that the world has been created by thought and is still ceaselessly being created in this
manner is the belief that can alone fructify the actual inner
practice of thought.

It is always the denial of the spiritual in the world that
produces the worst kind of malpractice in thought, even in

the field of science. Consider, for example, the theory that our planetary system arose from a primordial nebula that began to rotate and then densified into a central body from which rings and globes detached themselves, thus mechanically bringing into existence the entire solar system. Anyone who propounds this theory is committing a grave error of thought.

A simple experiment used to be made in the schools to demonstrate this theory. A drop of oil was made to float in a glass of water. The drop was then pierced with a pin and made to rotate. As a result, tiny globules of oil were thrown off from the central drop creating a miniature planetary system, thus proving to the pupil—so the teacher thought—that this planetary system could come into existence through a purely mechanical process.

Only impractical thought can draw such conclusions from this little experiment, for those who would apply this theory to the cosmos have forgotten one thing that it ordinarily might be well to forget occasionally and that is themselves. They forget that they have themselves brought this whole thing into rotation. If they had not been there and conducted the whole experiment, the separation of the little globules from the large drop would never have occurred. Had this fact been observed and applied logically to the cosmic system, they then would have been using complete healthy thinking. Similar errors of thought play a great part especially in science. Such things are far more important than people generally believe.

Considering the real practice of thought, it must be realized that thoughts can only be drawn from a world in which they already exist. Just as water can only be taken from a glass that actually contains water, so thoughts can only be extracted from things within which these thoughts are concealed. The world is built by thought, and only for this reason can thought be extracted from it. Were it otherwise, practical thought could not arise. When people can feel the full truth of these words, it will be easy for them to dispense with abstract thought. If they can confidently believe that thoughts are concealed behind the things around them, and that the actual facts of life take their course in obedience to thought—if they feel this, they will easily be converted to a practical habit of thinking based on truth and reality.

Let us now look at that practice of thinking that is of special importance to those who stand upon an anthroposophical foundation. The one who is convinced that the world of facts is born of thought will grasp the importance of the development of right thinking.

People who wish to fructify their thinking to such a degree that it will always take the right course in life must be guided by the following rules and must understand that these are actual, practical, and fundamental principles. If they will try again and again to shape their thinking according to these rules, certain effects will result. Their thinking will become practical even though at first it may not seem so. Other additional mental experiences of quite a different kind also will come to those who apply these fundamental principles.

They can begin by observing, as accurately as possible, something accessible in the outer world—for instance, the weather. They can watch the configuration of the clouds in the evening, the conditions at sunset, and so on, and mentally retain an exact picture of what has been observed. They should try to keep the picture in all its details before themselves for some time and endeavor to preserve as much of it as possible until the next day. At some time the next day they should again make a study of the weather conditions and again endeavor to gain an exact picture of them.

If in this manner they have pictured to themselves exactly the sequential order of the weather conditions, they will become distinctly aware that their thinking gradually becomes richer and more intense. For what makes thought impractical is the tendency to ignore details when observing a sequence of events in the world and to retain but a vague, general impression of them. What is of value, what is essential and fructifies thinking, is just this ability to form exact pictures, especially of successive events, so that one can say, "Yesterday it was like that; today it is like this." Thus, one calls up as graphically as possible an inner image of the two juxtaposed scenes that lie apart in the outer world.

This is, so to speak, nothing else but a certain expression of confidence in the thoughts that underlie reality. Those experimenting ought not to draw any conclusions immediately or to deduce from today's observation what kind of weather they might have tomorrow. That would corrupt their thinking. Instead, they must confidently feel that the things of outer reality are definitely related to one another and that tomorrow's events are somehow connected with those of today. But they must not speculate on these things. They must first inwardly re-think the sequence of the outer events as exactly as possible in mental pictures, and then place these images side by side, allowing them to melt into one another. This is a definite rule of thought that must be followed by those who wish to develop factual thinking. It is particularly advisable that this principle be practiced on those very things that are not yet understood and the inner connection of which has not yet been penetrated.

Therefore, the experimenter must have the confidence that such events of which he or she as yet has no understanding—the weather, for instance—and which in the outer world are connected with one another, will bring about inner connections. This must be done only in pictures, while refraining from thinking. The person must say inwardly, "I do not yet know what the relation is, but I shall let these things grow within me and if I refrain from speculation they will bring something about in me." It can be readily believed that something may take place in the invisible members of a person's nature if exact inner images of succeeding events are formed and at the same time all thinking is restrained.

The vehicle of a human being's thought life is the astral body.[1] As long as the human being is engaged in speculative thinking, this astral body is the slave of the ego. This conscious activity, however, does not occupy the astral body exclusively because the latter is also related in a certain manner to the whole cosmos.

---

1. For a full explanation of this and other anthroposophical terminology see Rudolf Steiner *Theosophy, An Introduction to the Spiritual Processes in Human Life and in the Cosmos* (Hudson, NY: Anthroposophic Press, 1994).

Now, to the extent we restrain arbitrary thinking and simply form mental pictures of successive events, to that extent do the inner thoughts of the world act within us and imprint themselves, without our being aware of it, on our astral body. To the extent we insert ourselves into the course of the world through observation of the events in the world and receive these images into our thoughts with the greatest possible clarity, allowing them to work within us, to that extent do those members of our organism that are withdrawn from our consciousness become ever more intelligent. If, in the case of inwardly connected events, we have once acquired the faculty of letting the new picture melt into the preceding one in the same way that the transition occurred in nature, it shall be found after a time that our thinking has gained considerable flexibility.

This is the procedure to be followed in matters not yet understood. Things, however, that are understood—events of everyday life, for example—should be treated in a somewhat different manner.

Let us presume that someone, perhaps our neighbor, had done this or that. We think about it and ask ourselves why he did it. We decide he has perhaps done it in preparation for something he intends to do the next day. We do not go any further but clearly picture his act and try to form an image of what he may do, imagining that the next day he will perform such and such an act. Then we wait to see what he really does since he may or may not do what we expected of him. We take note of what does happen and correct our thoughts accordingly. Thus, events of the present are chosen that are followed in thought into the future. Then we wait to see what actually happens.

This can be done either with actions involving people or something else. Whenever something is understood, we try to form a thought picture of what in our opinion will take place. If our opinion proves correct, our thinking is justified and all is well. If, however, something different from our expectation occurs, we review our thoughts and try to discover our mistake. In this way we try to correct our erroneous thinking by calm observation and examination of our errors. An attempt is made to find the reason for things occurring as they did. If we are right, however, we must be especially careful not to boast of our prediction and say, "Oh well, I knew yesterday that this would happen!"

This is again a rule based upon confidence that there is an inner necessity in things and events, that in the facts themselves there slumbers something that moves things. What is thus working within these things from one day to another are thought forces, and we gradually become conscious of them when meditating on things. By such exercises these thought forces are called up into our consciousness and if what has been thus foreseen is fulfilled, we are in tune with them. We have then established an inner relation with the real thought activity of the matter itself. So we train ourselves to think, not arbitrarily, but according to the inner necessity and the inner nature of the things themselves.

But our thinking can also be trained in other directions. An occurrence of today is also linked to what happened yesterday. We might consider a naughty child, for example, and ask ourselves what may have caused this behavior. The events are traced back to the previous day and the unknown cause hypothesized by saying to ourselves, "Since this occurred today, I must believe that it was prepared by this or that event that occurred yesterday or perhaps the day before."

We then find out what had actually occurred and so discover whether or not our thought was correct. If the true cause has been found, very well. But if our conclusion was wrong, then we should try to correct the mistake, find out how our thought process developed, and how it ran its course in reality.

To practice these principles is the important point. Time must be taken to observe things as though we were inside the things themselves with our thinking. We should submerge ourselves in the things and enter into their inner thought activity. If this is done, we gradually become aware of the fact that we are growing together with things. We no longer feel that they are outside us and we are here inside our shell thinking about them. Instead we come to feel as if our own thinking occurred within the things themselves. When a person has succeeded to a high degree in doing this, many things will become clear.

Goethe was such a man. He was a thinker who always lived with his thought within the things themselves. The psychologist Heinroth's book in 1826, *Anthropology*, characterized Goethe's thought as "objective." Goethe himself appreciated this characterization. What was meant is that such thinking does not separate itself from things, but remains within them. It moves within the necessity of things. Goethe's thinking was at the same time perception, and his perception was thinking. He had developed this way of thinking to a remarkable degree. More than once it occurred that, when he had planned to do something, he would go to the window and remark to the person who happened to be with him, "In three hours we shall have rain!" And so it would happen. From the little patch of sky he could see from the window he was able to foretell the weather conditions for the next few hours. His true thinking, remaining within the objects, thus enabled him to sense the coming event preparing itself in the preceding one.

Much more can actually be accomplished through practical thinking than is commonly supposed. When people have made these principles of thinking their own, they will notice that their thinking really becomes practical, that their horizon widens, and that they can grasp the things of the world in quite a different way. Gradually their attitude toward things and other people will change completely. An actual process will take place within them that will alter their whole conduct. It is of immense importance that they try to grow into the things in this way with their thinking, for it is in the most eminent sense a practical undertaking to train one's thinking by such exercises.

There is another exercise that is to be practiced especially by those to whom the right idea usually does not occur at the right time.

Such people should try above all things to stop their thinking from being forever influenced and controlled by the ordinary course of worldly events and whatever else may come with them. As a rule, when a person lies down for half an hour's rest, his thoughts are allowed to play freely in a thousand different directions, or on the other hand he may become absorbed with some trouble in his life. Before he realizes it such things will have crept into his consciousness and claimed his entire attention. If this habit persists, such a person will never experience the occasion when the right idea occurs to him at the right moment.

If he really wants this to happen, he must say inwardly whenever he can spare a half hour for rest, "Whenever I can spare the time, I will think about something I myself have chosen and I will bring it into my consciousness arbitrarily of my own free will. For example, I will think of something that occurred two years ago during a walk. I will deliberately recall what occurred then and I will think about it if only for five minutes. During these five minutes I will banish everything else from my mind and will myself choose the subject about which I wish to think."

He need not even choose so difficult a subject as this one. The point is not at all to change one's mental process through difficult exercises, but to get away from the ordinary routine of life in one's thinking. He must think of something quite apart from what enmeshes him during the ordinary course of the day. If nothing occurs to him to think about, he might open a book at random and occupy his thoughts with whatever first catches his eye. Or he may choose to think of something he saw at a particular time that morning on his way to work and to which he would otherwise have paid no attention. The main point is that it should be something totally different from the ordinary run of daily events, something that otherwise would not have occupied his thoughts.

If such exercises are practiced systematically again and again, it will soon be noticed that ideas come at the right moments, and the right thoughts occur when needed.

Through these exercises thinking will become activated and mobile—something of immense importance in practical life.

Let us consider another exercise that is especially helpful in improving one's memory.

One tries at first in the crude way people usually recall past events to remember something that occurred, let us say, yesterday. Such recollections are, as a rule, indistinct and colorless, and most people are satisfied if they can just remember a person's name. But if it is desired to develop one's memory, one can no longer be content with this. This must be clear. The following exercise must be systematically practiced, saying to oneself, "I shall recall exactly the person I saw yesterday, also the street corner where I met him, and what happened to be in his vicinity. I shall draw the whole picture as exactly as possible and shall even imagine the color and cut of his coat and vest." Most people will find themselves utterly incapable of doing this and will quickly see how much is lacking in their recollections to produce a really lifelike, graphic picture of what they met and experienced only yesterday.

Since this is true in the majority of cases, we must begin with that condition in which many people are unable to recollect their most recent experiences. It is only too true that most people's observations of things and events are usually inaccurate and vague. The results of a test given by a professor in one of the universities demonstrated that out of thirty students who took the test, only two had observed an occurrence correctly; the remaining twenty-eight reported it inaccurately. But a good memory is the child of accurate observation. A reliable memory is attained, let me repeat, by accurate observation and it can also be said that in a certain roundabout way of the soul it is born as the child of exact observation.

But if somebody cannot at first accurately remember his experiences of yesterday, what should he do? First, he should try to remember as accurately as he can what actually occurred. Where recollections fail he should fill in the picture with something incorrect that was not really present. The essential point here is that the picture be complete. Suppose it was forgotten whether or not someone was wearing a brown or a black coat. Then he might be pictured in a brown coat and brown trousers with such and such buttons on his vest and a yellow necktie. One might further imagine a general situation in which there was a yellow wall, a tall man passing on the left, a short one on the right, and so on.

All that can be remembered he puts into this picture, and what cannot be remembered is added imaginatively in order to have a completed mental picture. Of course, it is at first incorrect but through the effort to create a complete picture he is induced to observe more accurately. Such exercises must be continued, and although they might be tried and failed fifty times, perhaps the fifty-first time he shall be able to remember accurately what the person he has met looked like, what he wore, and even little details like the buttons on his vest. Then nothing will be overlooked and every detail will imprint itself on his memory. Thus he will have first sharpened his powers of observation by these exercises and in addition, as the fruit of this accurate observation, he will have improved his memory.

He should take special care to retain not only names and main features of what he wishes to remember, but also to retain vivid images covering all the details. If he cannot remember some detail, he must try for the time being to fill in the picture and thus make it a whole. He will then notice that his memory, as though in a roundabout way, slowly becomes reliable. Thus it can be seen how definite direction can be given for making thinking increasingly more practical.

There is still something else that is of particular importance. In thinking about some matters we feel it necessary to come to a conclusion. We consider how this or that should be done and then make up our minds in a certain way. This inclination, although natural, does not lead to practical thinking. All overly hasty thinking does not advance us but sets us back. Patience in these things is absolutely essential.

Suppose, for instance, we desire to carry out some particular plan. There are usually several ways that this might be done. Now we should have the patience first to imagine how things would work out if we were to execute our plan in one way and then we should consider what the results would be of doing it in another. Surely there will always be reasons for preferring one method over another but we should refrain from forming an immediate decision. Instead, an attempt should be made to imagine the two possibilities and then we must say to ourselves, "That will do for the present; I shall now stop thinking about his matter." No doubt there are people who will become fidgety at this point, and although it is difficult to overcome such a condition, it is extremely useful to do so. It then becomes possible to imagine how the matter might be handled in two ways, and to decide to stop thinking about it for awhile.

Whenever it is possible, action should be deferred until the next day, and the two possibilities considered again at that time. You will find that in the interim conditions have changed and that the next day you will be able to form a different, or at least a more thorough decision than could have been reached the day before. An inner necessity is hidden in things and if we do not act with arbitrary impatience but allow this inner necessity to work in us—and it will—we shall find the next day that it has enriched our thinking, thus making possible a wiser decision. This is exceedingly valuable.

We might, for example, be asked to give our advice on a problem and to make a decision. But let us not thrust forward our decision immediately. We should have the patience to place the various possibilities before ourselves without forming any definite conclusions, and we then should quietly let these possibilities work themselves out within us. Even the popular proverb says that one should sleep over a matter before making a decision.

To sleep over it is not enough, however. It is necessary to consider two or, better still, several possibilities that will continue to work within us when our ego is not consciously occupied with them. Later on, when we return again to the matter in question, it will be found that certain thought forces have been stirred up within us in this manner, and that as a result our thinking has become more factual and practical.

It is certain that what a person seeks can always be found in the world, whether standing at the carpenter's bench, or following the plough, or belonging to one of the professions. If he will practice these exercises, he will become a practical thinker in the most ordinary matters of everyday life. If he thus trains himself, he will approach and look at the things of the world in a quite different manner from previously. Although at first these exercises may seem related only to one's own innermost life, they are entirely applicable and of the greatest importance precisely for the outer world. They have powerful consequences.

An example will demonstrate how necessary it is to think about things in a really practical manner. Let us imagine that for some reason or other a man climbs a tree. He falls from the tree, strikes the ground, and is picked up dead. Now, the thought most likely to occur to us is that the fall killed him. We would be inclined to say that the fall was the cause and death the effect. In this instance cause and effect seem logically connected. But this assumption may completely confuse the true sequence of facts, for the man may have fallen as a consequence of heart failure. To the observer the external event is exactly the same in both cases. Only when the true causes are known can a correct judgment be formed. In this case it might have been that the man was already dead before he fell and the fall had nothing to do with his death. It is thus possible to invert completely cause and effect. In this instance the error is evident, but often they are not so easily discernible. The frequency with which such errors in thinking occur is amazing. Indeed, it must be said that in the field of science conclusions in which this confusion of cause and effect is permitted are being drawn every day. Most people do not grasp this fact, however, because they are not acquainted with the possibilities of thinking.

Still another example will show you clearly how such

errors in thinking arise and how a person who has been practicing exercises like these can no longer make such mistakes. Suppose someone concludes that human beings as they are today are descendants of the ape. This means that what that person has come to know in the ape—the forces active in this animal—have attained higher perfection and a human being is the result. Now, to show the meaning of this theory in terms of thought, let us imagine that this person is the only human being on earth, and that there are only those apes present that, according to his theory, can evolve into human beings. He now studies these apes with the utmost accuracy down to the most minute detail and then forms a concept of what lives in them. Excluding himself and without ever having seen another human being let him now try to develop the concept of a man solely from his concept of the ape. He will find this to be quite impossible. His concept "ape" will never transform itself into the concept "human being."

If he had cultivated correct habits of thinking, this man would have said to himself, "My concept of the ape does not change into the concept of man. What I perceive in the ape, therefore, can never become a human being, otherwise my concept would have to change likewise. There must be something else present that I am unable to perceive." So he would have to imagine an invisible, supersensible entity behind the physical ape that he would be unable to perceive but that alone would make the ape's transformation into a human being a possible conception.

We shall not enter into a discussion of the impossibility of this case, but simply point out the erroneous thinking underlying this theory. If this man had thought correctly he would have seen that he could not possibly conceive of such a theory without assuming the existence of something supersensible. Upon further investigation you will discover that an overwhelmingly large number of people have committed this error of thinking. Errors like these, however, will no longer occur to those who have trained their thinking as suggested here.

For anyone capable of thinking correctly a large part of modern literature (especially that of the sciences) becomes a source of unpleasant experience. The distorted and misguided thinking expressed in it can cause even physical pain in a person who has to work through it. It should be understood, however, that this is not said with any intent to slight the wealth of observation and discovery that has been accumulated by modern natural science and its objective methods of research.

Now let us consider "shortsighted" thinking. Most people are unconscious of the fact that their thinking is not factual, but that it is for the most part only the result of thought habits. The decisions and conclusions therefore of a person whose thought penetrates the world and life will differ greatly from those of one whose ability to think is limited or nil. Consider the case of a materialistic thinker. To convince such a person through reasoning, however logical, sound, and good, is not an easy task. It is usually a useless effort to try to convince a person with little knowledge of life through reason. Such a person does not see the reasons that make this or that statement valid and possible if the habit has been formed of seeing nothing but matter in everything and simply adhering to this habit of thinking.

Today it can generally be said that people are not prompted by reasons when making statements but rather by the thinking habits behind these reasons. They have acquired habits of thought that influence all their feelings and sensations, and when reasons are put forth, they are simply the mask of the habitual thinking that screens these feelings and sensations. Not only is the wish often the father of the thought, but it can also be said that all our feelings and mental habits are the parents of our thoughts. Someone who knows life knows how difficult it is to convince another person by means of logical reasoning. What really decides and convinces lies much deeper in the human soul.

There are good reasons for the existence of the Anthroposophical Movement and for the activities in its various branches. Everyone participating in the work of the Movement for any length of time comes to notice that they have acquired a new way of thinking and feeling. For the work in the various branches is not merely confined to finding logical reasons for things. A new and more comprehensive quality of feeling and sensation is also developed.

How some people scoffed a few years ago when they heard their first lectures in spiritual science. Yet today how many things have become self-evident to these same people who previously looked upon these things as impossible absurdities. In working in the Anthroposophical Movement one not only learns to modify one's thinking, one also learns to unfold a wider perspective of soul life.

We must understand that our thoughts derive their coloring from far greater depths than are generally imagined. It is our feelings that frequently impel us to hold certain opinions. The logical reasons that are put forward are often a mere screen or mask for our deeper feelings and habits of thinking.

To bring ourselves to a point at which logical reasons themselves possess a real significance for us, we must have learned to love logic itself. Only when we have learned to love factuality and objectivity will logical reason be decisive for us. We should gradually learn to think objectively, not allowing ourselves to be swayed by our preference for this or that thought. Only then will our vision broaden in the sense that we do not merely follow the mental ruts of others but in such a way that the reality of the things themselves will teach us to think correctly.

True practicality is born of objective thinking, that is, thinking that flows into us from the things themselves. It is only by practicing such exercises as have just been described that we learn to take our thoughts from things. To do these exercises properly we should choose to work with sound and wholesome subjects that are least affected by our culture. These are the objects of nature.

To train our thinking using the things of nature as objects to think about will make really practical thinkers of us. Once we have trained ourselves in the practical use of this fundamental principle, our thinking, we shall be able to handle the most everyday occupations in a practical way. By training the human soul in this way a practical viewpoint is developed in our thinking.

The fruit of the Anthroposophical Movement must be to place really practical thinkers in life. What we have come to believe is not of as much importance as the fact that we should become capable of surveying with understanding the things around us. That spiritual science should penetrate our souls, thereby stimulating us to inner soul activity and expanding our vision, is of far more importance than merely theorizing about what extends beyond the things of the senses into the spiritual. In this, anthroposophy is truly practical.

Overcoming Nervousness:

Nervousness and I–ness

Introduction

In this lecture, Rudolf Steiner introduces a principle that sets his approach apart from many spiritual and psychological techniques. This principle is psychic hierarchy: that each level of a human's being should inform, from above, the level just beneath it. All psychic distress, Steiner implies, derives from a breakdown in such hierarchy. The fundamental insight here, distinctive of anthroposophy, is that lower, even diseased, aspects of the mind are in fact transformations and degenerations of something august. Emerson wrote, "Our being is descending into us from we know not whence"—with *descending* as the operative term. What we know only too well, how anxious and afraid we are, how out of sorts, can be recognized as the fallen form of a high spiritual essence.

The original German title of the essay encapsulates Steiner's concept of hierarchy in a simple binary formula: *Nervositaet und Ichheit*, or "Nervousness and I-hood." These two are the poles of our mental life: wherever I am active, nervousness cannot appear, for nervousness is made up precisely of the unused potential of the self. As a recently published record of angelic conversation put it, "Nervousness is being without goal."[1] The purpose

---

1. Gitta Mallasz, *Talking with Angels* (Einsiedeln: Daimon Verlag, 1988).

of Steiner's injunctions is to redirect us, so that our psyche's being regains its goal and its activity casts out nervousness. This process may be none other than what John meant by saying, "perfect love casteth out all fear."

If we examine how broadly Steiner uses the term "nervousness," and reflect that the word is a close sibling of "neurosis," we begin to realize Steiner's therapeutic scope, and the enormous implications of the "trivial" techniques and topics addressed here. What Freud attempted to do in psychoanalysis, Steiner achieved in anthroposophy from quite the opposite direction. Unlike Freud, who would conquer "neurosis" (a term that smells of formaldehyde and the hospital) by transforming the lower animal urges into higher egoic reflectivity, Steiner sought to expel "nervousness" (the lived experience of a misled life) by reorienting the soul to its divine origin.

In the years since Steiner and Freud died, nervousness has surely only increased its hold on Western people. So, too, have the psychotherapeutic techniques supposed to alleviate it. While many of these may be of dubious value, or even contribute to the problem, others may be effective. Certainly later authors have unknowingly recommended psychotherapeutic practices already suggested by Steiner. For example, the technique Steiner discusses of allowing inner voices to speak the pros and cons of a decision, and then oneself choosing among these voices, closely resembles the Gestalt "two chair" technique and its derivatives, such as the Voice Dialogue method of Harold Stone.[2] In

---

2. Harold Stone and Sidra Winkelman, *Embracing Our Selves* (San Rafael, CA: New World Library, 1989).

Stone's work, the client is guided to speak alternately out of many inner personas, thereby strengthening the central I in its supervisory role.

In this brief lecture, Steiner also finds time to foresee a number of visualization and cognitive/behavioral techniques "invented" in recent decades. Above and beyond these many hints, however, two further anticipations deserve special mention. Steiner's observation of the harmful effects of student "cramming" seems almost to have come from the same writer as Simone Weil's much later "Reflections on the Right Use of School Studies with a View to the Love of God."[3] In that essay, Weil emphasizes the importance of the attention, which is exercised all the more intensely when applied to something we do not find intrinsically interesting. She equates attention, as does Steiner in this lecture, with the essence of the human spirit.

Again, Steiner's lesson that we teach our children more by example than by precept has the ring of difficult truth. For who can change his or her behavior with the same ease as mouthing maxims? It is said that Mahatma Gandhi was approached by a mother with her young son. The mother begged Gandhi, "Gandhiji, please, my son eats too much sugar. It is not healthy. Tell him to stop." Gandhi replied, "Come back in three days." When in three days mother and son returned, Gandhi said to the boy, "Do not eat sugar. It is not good for you." And he bade them farewell. The boy's mother was grateful, but asked Gandhi why he had not given the simple advice three days before. "Three

3. George Panichas, ed., *The Simone Weil Reader* (New York: David McKay Co., 1977).

days ago," replied the saint, "I had not given up sugar myself." (Perhaps the most remarkable aspect of this story is that it took Gandhi only three days to know he had given up sugar.)

Anyone familiar with Steiner's writings and lectures will recognize in this lecture on nervousness a pervasive characteristic of his work: Steiner recommends many exercises. In fact, he recommends so many exercises that the reader is not merely unlikely to attempt them all, but unlikely to attempt a single one. Readers may feel swamped by such a deluge of recommendations, suggestions, techniques, and projects to be undertaken. This very overabundance, however, is the token of something quite wonderful, and altogether unusual both in traditional psychology and in New Age spiritual psychology. For Steiner, the psyche is alive. Its description cannot be pieced together from a finite number of component parts; its evolution cannot be accomplished or even delineated by a finite number of precepts. Its depths, as well as its heights, bristle with infinities. Therefore, whoever speaks from the psyche's own sources cannot offer limited viewpoints. We may taste, in Steiner's overabundance, something of the living water Christ offered to the Samaritan woman. And we may ask in wonder, as she did, "Sir, thou hast nothing to draw with, and the well is deep: from whence then hast thou that living water?"

Michael Lipson

Munich, January 11, 1912

THE SUGGESTIONS to be given today connect with much that we already know, but they can still be useful for one or another of us, and can even lead us into a more exact contemplation of the essence of the human being and of its connection with the world. The anthroposophist can very often hear all kinds of things from non-anthroposophists, apart from the many rebuttals and objections against spiritual science lately mentioned in the public lectures. For example, both learned and unlearned people object over and over again to our speaking, in spiritual science, about the division of the whole human being into those four members that we always bring up: physical body, ether—or life—body, astral body, and the I. And then doubters can object, so to speak: Well, maybe that's how it is for someone who has developed certain hidden forces of the soul; maybe such a person can see this composition of the human being; but someone who doesn't see such things, can have no reason to turn toward such a viewpoint. However, we must emphasize that, if one is attentive to human life, this life in a certain sense can give corroborations of what spirit-knowledge has to say. Further, if one applies what one can learn from spirit-knowledge to one's life, then such an application proves extraordinarily useful. And one soon finds that this usefulness (I don't mean here usefulness in a low sense, but usefulness that is of use for life in the most beautiful sense) can gradually give us a kind of conviction, even if we do not want to enter into what clairvoyant perception offers.

It is only too well known that in our time people complain often of what we can encompass with the much-feared word "nervousness." And we would not be surprised in the least if someone feels driven to say: In our time, there is really no one left who is not nervous about *something.* How understandable this statement is, in a certain way! Quite apart from the social relationships and conditions to which we can ascribe this or that cause for this nervousness, the nervous conditions, as we have characterized them, are there. They express themselves in life in the most varied ways; they express themselves, as we could perhaps say, in the lightest way, in the least uncomfortable way, when a person becomes what we could call a will-o'-the-wisp of the soul. This is the name I would give to someone who is incapable of holding onto a thought properly, and pursuing its consequences in a real way. Such people hop from one thought to another; if you want to hold them in one place they have already long ago gone somewhere else. A hastiness of the soul life—this is often the lightest form of nervousness.

Another kind of nervousness is that of people who don't know what to do with themselves; when things require a decision from them they cannot decide, and never really know for sure what they should do in this or that situation.

And then these conditions can lead on to other, already more serious cases, such that this nervousness lives itself out gradually more and more in actual forms of disease, for which, perhaps, one can cite no organic cause. These forms of disease sometimes mimic organic diseases in a deceptive way, so that one could believe the person has, perhaps, a serious stomach ailment, but really suffers only from what one can sum up, even if trivially and without much meaning, under the word "nervousness." And countless other conditions: who among us is not familiar with them? Who does not suffer from them, either because we have them ourselves or because others in our environment have them. One need not go so far as to speak about the great events of outer life as a "political alcoholism," but people have spoken in recent days about that kind of nervous activity in public life as a kind of conduct that otherwise only expresses itself in an individual who has been infected somewhat by alcoholism. The word is appropriate for the way political affairs have been conducted in Europe over the last months. One also sees in outward life something about which one could say: here too, one notices not only that nervousness is present, but that people sense it in a certain connection as something quite unpleasant. Everywhere, then, something like nervousness is present.

All this will, in the near future, grow worse and worse for people. If people remain as they are, then a good outlook for the future cannot by any means be offered. For there are harmful influences that affect our current life in a quite extraordinary way and that carry over from one person to the other like an epidemic. Therefore people become a bit diseased in this direction: not only the ones who have the illness, but also others, who are perhaps only weak but otherwise healthy, get it by a kind of infection.

It is enormously harmful for our time that a great number of the people who arrive in prominent public positions study in the way that people study at present. There are actually whole branches of study in which one lives, let us say, the whole year at the university doing things other than thinking through and studying through what the professors are saying; one goes into lectures now and then, but what one really wants to learn is acquired in a few weeks— that is to say, people cram. The bad part is the cramming. And since in a certain regard this cramming goes as far as to the lower grades, the ills that come from it are by no means inconsiderable. The essential part of this cramming is that there is no real connection of the soul-interest, of the innermost kernel of being, with what one crams. In the schools, the reigning opinion among the students is even: Oh, if only I could now forget what I have just learned! So that vehement wanting to possess what one learns is not present. A slight chain of interest links the human soul kernel with what people take in.

Now people can be made fit in this way, in a certain regard, to take a hand in public life, because they crammed, or learned, the thing they wanted to learn, but since they are not inwardly connected with it, they are far away in the soul from what they are doing with their head. And for the whole human being there is hardly anything worse than being far away in the soul, with one's heart, from what the head must perform. This not only goes against the nature of a finer, more sensitive person, but also influences the strength and energy of the human etheric body to the highest degree—precisely of the etheric body. The ether, or life, body becomes ever weaker from such activity, because of the slight connection that exists between the human soul kernel and what the person is doing. The more people have to do what does not interest them, the weaker they makes their ether body.

Anthroposophy, if acquired in a healthy way, should do more than teach people that a human being consists of physical body, ether body, and so forth; anthroposophy should also have the healthy effect of developing strongly these individual members within the human being.

Now if a person makes a very simple experiment, but repeats this experiment eagerly, then a triviality can actually work wonders. Forgive me if today I speak just of individual observations, of trivialities, but these can become very significant for the life of the human being. For, intimately connected with what I have just characterized is the light forgetfulness that people sometimes show. Light forgetfulness is something unpleasant in life; anthroposophy can, however, show us that this forgetfulness is damaging to health in the most eminent sense. And, strange as it may sound, it is true that many outbreaks of human nature that border on being very diseased would be avoided if people were less forgetful. Now, you can say, they *are* forgetful; indeed, who can say (as we realize if we have an overview of life) that they are completely free of forgetfulness? Take a really trivial case: a person discovers he is forgetful in that he never knows where he has put the things he uses. This is something that happens in life, isn't it? One person cannot find the cufflinks that he put down the evening before, another can never find her pencil, and so on. It seems strange and banal to talk about these things, but they do happen in life. And precisely from observation of what we can learn in anthroposophy, there is a good exercise for gradually improving this condition of forgetfulness.

Here is the very simple technique: now let us assume a lady puts down, say, her brooch or a man puts down his cufflinks somewhere in the evening, and, when they cannot find these objects the next morning, they realize their tendency to forgetfulness. Now you could say, yes, certainly, and one can accustom oneself to always putting them down in the same place. That won't be possible for all objects. However, we do not want to speak at the moment of this particular means of curing oneself, but rather of a much more effective means. Namely, assume that a person who notices a tendency to forgetfulness, immediately says inwardly, I now want to place the objects in very different spots, but I want never to place an object in a specific spot without also developing the thought when I put it down: I have placed this object in this spot! Then one tries to imprint in oneself an image of the surroundings. Let us assume we place a safety pin at the edge of a table at the corner. We lay it down with the thought: I am laying down this pin on this edge and I imprint the right angle around it as a picture, such that the pin is surrounded on two sides by edges, and so on, and I go calmly away from the place. And I will see that even if it doesn't work out right away in every case, if I make this practice a rule then my forgetfulness will fall away from me more and more. It depends on a very specific thought being formulated, namely the thought: I am laying the pin down there. I have brought my I into connection with what I am carrying out, and besides that I have added something in the way of a picture. Pictoriality in thinking what I myself am doing, and besides this pictorial mental imaging, I bring the fact into connection with the kernel of my essence. This bringing together with the soul-spiritual kernel of essence, as addressed with the little word "I," along with pictoriality, can sharpen our memory quite fundamentally. In this way we have something useful for life, since we become less forgetful. Perhaps we would not make so much of it if that were all that could be achieved. But much more can be achieved in this way.

Let us assume that it became a custom among people to evoke such thoughts when they lay down certain objects— then this custom alone would evoke a strengthening of the human ether body. The human ether body is in fact more and more consolidated by doing this kind of thing; it becomes ever stronger and stronger. We have learned from anthroposophy that the ether, or life, body must be for us in a certain sense the bearer of the memory. If we do something that strengthens the powers of memory, then we can understand right away that such a strengthening of the powers of memory aids our ether body. As anthroposophists we need not be so very surprised about it. But suppose you suggest to someone who not only is forgetful, but also shows certain conditions of nervousness, what has been described here. If the restless or nervous person does this—accompanies the placement of objects with such thoughts—then you will see that he or she not only becomes less forgetful, but also gradually, through the strengthening of the ether body, puts aside certain so-called nervous conditions. Then a proof will have been provided, through life, that what we say about the ether body is right. For if we behave in the corresponding way toward the ether body, it definitely shows that it assumes these forces; so what we say about it is correct. Life proves, in such a case, that this is extraordinarily important.

Another matter, which once again can seem to be a triviality, but which is extraordinarily important! You know that what we can call the physical body and the ether body border immediately on one another in the human being. The ether body is immediately contained within the physical. Now, today, you can make an observation that is not so very rare at all, an observation whose validity is not known to those people about whom we make the observation. When we make this observation and bear within us a healthy, compassionate soul, then we will have, precisely, compassion for these people we are observing. Have you seen, for example, people writing at the post office counter who make very peculiar movements before they begin to write a letter—before they begin to write a *B*, for instance. First they make some movements in the air and then begin! Or it need not even go so far; for this is already the indication of a serious condition, if people are forced through their jobs to do such things; it may merely go so far that the people—watch them sometime—have to give themselves a little jolt, so to speak, with each stroke, and in fact they write jaggedly, not going up and down evenly, but jaggedly. You can see it in the handwriting in this way.

From spiritual scientific knowledge we can understand such a condition in the following way: For a completely healthy human being—healthy in regard to the physical body and ether body—the ether body, which is directed by the astral body, must always be able to take absolute hold of the physical body, and the physical body must everywhere,

in all its movements, be able to become a servant of the
ether body. If the physical body moves on its own, beyond
what the soul can really want—that is, what the astral body
can really want—then it is an unhealthy condition, a pre-
ponderance of the physical body over the etheric body. And
in everyone who has the conditions just described, we once
again have to do with a weakness of the etheric body, which
consists in its no longer being able fully to control the physical body. This relationship of the etheric body to the physical body even lies, occultly, at the base of all conditions of
cramping, which are fundamentally connected in that the
etheric body exercises a lesser command over the physical
body than it should exercise, so that the physical dominates
and carries out all kinds of movements on its own. Mean-
while the human being is healthy in relation to the fullness
of its being only if everything that it does is subordinate to
the will of the astral body.

Now here again there is a possibility, if this condition has
not gained too much the upper hand, of helping people:
only one must reckon with the occult facts. One has to
reckon with the need for the etheric body as such to be
strengthened. One must to a certain extent believe in the
existence and effective capacity of the ether body. Suppose
an unfortunate man has so ruined himself that he continually makes restless motions with his fingers before he begins
to write this or that letter. Now it will be good in all circumstances to advise the person: All right, take a vacation
and write less for a while, and you will get better! But this
advice is only a halfway advice; one could do much more if
one also gave the person another suggestion, the second
half of the advice: And try, without making a lot of

effort—a quarter or a half hour every day are enough—try to take on a different handwriting, to change your writing style, so that you are required not to write mechanically, as you have up until now, but to pay attention! Whereas you used to write the *F* in that way, now write it steeper and in a quite different form, so that you must pay attention! Accustom yourself to painting the letters.

If spiritual knowledge were more widespread, then when such a person came back from vacation and had acquired a new handwriting style, his superiors would not say, "What kind of nutty guy are you, you write completely differently!" People would realize that this is a fundamental curative technique. For we are forced, when we change our writing in this way, to be attentive to what we are doing. And to be attentive to what we are doing always means to bring the innermost kernel of our being into intimate connection with the matter at hand. And everything, in turn, that brings the innermost kernel of our being into connection with what we do, strengthens our ether body. In this way we become healthy human beings. It would be good to work on a certain strengthening of the ether body systematically in upbringing and in school, so that it occurs even in youth. Here what anthroposophy suggests today will not be carried out for a long time, because the authorities in question will count anthroposophy as something strange for a long time; but it doesn't matter. Let us assume that in teaching children to write, we first teach them a certain style of writing, and then, after a few years, we simply change the writing style without any other reason than to do so. Then the change in handwriting and the strengthening of the attention that would have to come about during the change would have an enormously strengthening influence on the developing ether body, and many of the nervous conditions people have would not come up.

So you see that one can do something in life that strengthens the ether body, and this is of extraordinary importance. For it is precisely the weakness of the ether body that leads to the numerous really unhealthy situations in the present time. It can even be said—and truly, it is not saying too much—that certain forms of disease, which may very well be based in things about which nothing can be done, would run a very different course if the ether body were stronger than they run in the case of a weakened ether body, which is a standard feature of contemporary humanity. With this we have pointed to something that can be referred to as working on the ether body. We apply certain things to the ether body. One cannot apply anything at all to something that isn't there, something that can be denied. By showing that it is useful to do certain things with the etheric body, and by being able to prove that these things have an effect, one is showing that something like the etheric body does exist. Everywhere life offers the appropriate proofs of what anthroposophy has to give us.

Our etheric body can also grow fundamentally stronger if we do something else to improve our memory. Perhaps in another connection this has already been mentioned here. But for all forms of disease in which nervousness plays a part, one should certainly take advice drawn from this area as well. That is, one can do an enormous amount to strengthen the etheric body if one remembers the things one knows not only in the normal order one knows them but also remembering them backward. Let us say that in school someone has to learn a string of rulers or battles or other events. They are learned according to the year in which they occurred. It is extraordinarily good not only to have them learned or to learn them oneself in the normal order, but also to learn the matter in the reverse order, running through everything for oneself from back to front. This is an extraordinarily important matter. For if we do something like this in a more comprehensive way, we contribute once again to an enormous strengthening of our etheric body. To think through whole dramas backward to the beginning, or stories we have read, these are things that are important to the highest degree for the consolidation of the etheric body.

Now, you will be able to see that today people do not apply in life any of what we have just been discussing. In the contemporary restless racing of the day, we have very little chance to arrive at the inner peace that allows us to carry out such exercises. Normally a working person is too tired by evening to think any of the thoughts we have been discussing. But if spiritual science penetrates into people's hearts and souls, then they will realize that we could really do without an infinite amount of what goes on these days, and actually everyone can take the amount of time necessary for strengthening exercises of this kind. People would see very quickly, especially if they took pains with such things in the realm of education, that enormously favorable results are the consequences.

Let us mention another triviality, which to be sure is not so very useful in later life, but if a person has not cultivated it in early youth, then it is good to practice it in later life. That is to look again at certain things we accomplish, regardless of whether they leave a trace or not. This is relatively easy with regard to what we write. I am even convinced that many people could disabuse themselves of ugly handwriting if they tried, letter by letter, to look at what they have written, really to let their eyes pass again over what they have just written. This is possible to do quite well. But there is still another exercise that is very useful. That is, try to look at how we walk, how we move our hands, our head, how we laugh and so forth; in short, if we try to give ourselves a pictorial account of our gestures. Very few people (this is something you can realize if you observe life closely enough) know how they walk. Very few have an idea of how it looks to someone who notices this. But it is good to do some of that, to gain a mental picture of oneself. For if we apply this sort of thing in life we will doubtlessly correct much of what we do (as indicated, it must not be pursued too far or it contributes too much toward human vanity), but, apart from that, it can have an enormously favorable effect on the consolidation of the etheric body, and also on the control of the etheric body by the astral body. And when we observe our gestures, when we look at what we do, when we have a mental image of our deeds, the control of the etheric body by the astral body grows ever stronger and stronger. That is, we arrive at the point where we can even, if necessary, suppress something we do. As things stand, people are less and less able to suppress something habitual at will, or to do something differently. But one of the greatest achievements of the human being is the ability to do what one does differently at times.

We are not trying to establish a handwriting school here; these days people might want to learn to alter their hand-

writing only to use it dishonestly. But as long as one under-
takes to be perfectly honorable about it, it is good for the
consolidation of the etheric body to take on a different
handwriting. And in general it is good to acquire the ability
to do things one has planned in a different way, not to be set
on doing something only in one way. So we do not need to
be fanatical advocates of equal facility with both hands, but
if we nevertheless attempt in a moderate way to do certain
tasks with the left hand (we need not force it beyond what
we can really do), then this favorably influences the control
that our astral body should exercise over our etheric body.
Strengthening the human being in the way offered by spiritual scientific insight is something that should be brought to
our culture through the spread of spiritual science.

And in fact this is something of great import—it could be
called the cultivation of the will. Earlier we emphasized that
nervousness expresses itself precisely in the confusion people often feel today about how to set about doing what they
really wish to do or actually should wish to do. They draw
back from carrying out what they have undertaken; they
don't bring it off, and so on. This can be formulated as a
certain weakness of the will, and it is caused by a lack of
control of the astral body by the I. There is always insuffi-
cient control of the astral body by the I when this kind of
weakness of will appears; it is as if people simultaneously
want something and don't want it, or at least don't manage
to really carry out what they want. Many do not even manage to earnestly want what they want to want. Now, there is
a simple means to strengthen the will for the outer life. The
means is this: to suppress wishes that are doubtless there,
not to act on them, if non-action on the wishes is not harm-

ful and is possible. For if we examine ourselves in life, we find from morning to night countless things that we want, which it would be nice to have, but we also find many such wishes that we can forego, without harming someone else and without neglecting our own responsibilities: wishes whose satisfaction would give a certain pleasure, but which could also remain unsatisfied. If, then, one proceeds systematically, one can find among one's many wishes those of which it can be said, No, now I will not fulfill that wish. This is not to be done in the wrong way, but only with something that leads to no harm, whose fulfillment would bring nothing but comfort, happiness, pleasure. If one systematically suppresses wishes of this kind, then every suppression of a kind of wish means an increase in strength of will, in the strength of the I over the astral body. And if in later life we submit ourselves to such a procedure, then we will be able to make up, in this regard, for much that education currently neglects in many ways.

Now it is actually quite difficult to work effectively in this area, for one has to take into account that even if one, as a teacher, let's say, is in the position of being able to satisfy some emerging wish of a child or some young person, and refuses the wish, then not only a simple non-action may be set up, but also a kind of antipathy. But this can be harmful in a pedagogical sense, so that one could perhaps say: Yes, it looks doubtful whether one should introduce into one's educational principles the non-fulfillment of wishes of the students. One stands here before a real dilemma. If a father wants to educate his son by saying as often as possible, "No, Karl, you can't have that!", then he will more definitely evoke the boy's distaste for himself than he will achieve the good that is aimed at through non-fulfillment of wishes. The question arises: What is to be done? And one could simply not introduce such things at all.

But there is a very simple way to introduce it: One refuses the wishes, not to the young person, but to oneself, but in such a way that the young person is aware that one has foregone this or that. Now, in the first seven years of life, but even later as an aftereffect, a strong imitative drive is in effect, and we shall see, if we forego this or that in the presence of those we have to educate, that they imitate this, they see it as something worth striving for; and with this we will be doing something enormously significant.

So we see that our thoughts need only be led and directed in the right way through what spiritual science can be for us. Then spiritual science will not be theory; it will become life-wisdom, really something that supports us and carries us further in life.

An important means of strengthening the control of our I over the astral body can be learned to a certain extent from the two public lectures that I held here. [4] The special thing about these two lectures was that what could be said both for and against a thing was introduced. If you test how people position themselves in life in terms of their souls, you will see that generally when people have to act or think, they actually only say what can be said either for or against a

---

4. Given on January 8 and 10 in München: *Wie widerlegt man Theosophie?* [How does one refute Theosophy?] and *Wie begründet man Theosophy?* [How does one establish Theosophy?] These lectures were not fully transcribed and therefore are not included in the collected works. Parallel lectures were, however, given in Berlin and are printed in *Ergebnisse der Geistesforschung* [Results of Spiritual Research], (GA 62).

thing. That is the norm. But there is nothing in life that cannot be handled in such a way that there is both a *pro* and a *con*—nothing at all. There is a pro and a con for everything, and it is good if we accustom ourselves always to take into account not only the one but also the other, not only the pro *or* the con, but also the pro *and* the con. Even for things that we then actually do, it is good to present to oneself why we would do better under certain circumstances not to do it or simply, if it is better to do it, to make clear to oneself that there are also reasons against doing it.

Vanity generally contradicts the notion that one should bring up the counter arguments against what one does, since people want only too much to be purely good. A person can seem to offer proof of being a good person by saying, I only do what there are good reasons for. And it is uncomfortable to realize that there are also many objections for almost everything that one does in life. We are really—I say it because it is extraordinarily important for life—not at all as good as we think. But this generalization has little purpose; it only has a purpose if in the individual things one does, despite carrying them out, since life does demand them, one also considers what could lead us to forego them. What this achieves can be presented to our soul in the following simple way: You will certainly have already encountered people who are weak-willed in the sense that they would rather not decide anything for themselves, but always prefer that the other person make the decision for them, so that they only have to carry out what they are supposed to do. They dump the responsibility, so to speak, and prefer to ask what they are supposed to do instead of finding the reasons for this or that action by themselves. Now, I do not introduce this case in order to present it as important in itself, but to achieve something else.

Let us take a person of this kind, who likes to ask others—mind you, what I have said is something that can be easily objected to, as well as assented to; one can hardly utter anything in life that couldn't be refuted in some fashion. Let us take such a person confronting two people who give advice on the same issue. One says, Yes!; the other says, Don't do it! Then we will experience in life that one adviser wins out over the other adviser. The one who has a stronger influence on that person's will wins out over the other. What kind of phenomenon is this really? As insignificant as it seems, it is a highly significant phenomenon. If I stand before two people, one of whom says yes, the other no, and I carry out the yes, then that will works on in me, that strength of will has made itself felt in such a way that it empowered me to my action. One person's strength of will won out in me over the other person; the strength of that human being was victorious in me.

Now, assume that I am not standing before two other people, one of whom says yes and the other no, but that I stand there quite alone and bring out for myself the yes or no in my own heart, and bring up the reasons for each one; no one else comes to me, but I myself bring up the reasons for and against the matter. That develops a strong power, but now it is within myself. What earlier was exercised in me by the other person, I have now developed for myself as a strength within my soul. So if I pose a choice to myself inwardly, I allow a strength to conquer a weakness. And this is enormously important, because this again strengthens the control of the I over the astral body tremendously. Now we should not regard this as something unpleasant—to really honestly test the pros and cons in every individual case, wherever possible—and if we attempt to carry out what we have been describing, we will then see that a great deal has been achieved toward the strengthening the will.

But the issue also has a shadow side, namely that instead of a strengthening of the will, a weakening can emerge. This occurs if, after evaluating the pros and cons for oneself, one then does not act under the influence of one or the other power, but rather does nothing at all, out of negligence, following neither the one way nor the other. It seems then that one has obeyed the no, but really one has simply been lazy. Consequently, it is a good idea not to proceed with the self-presentation of pros and cons when you are tired, nor in any way worn out, but only when you feel strong, so that you know: I am not worn out, I can really follow through with the reason for presenting the pros and cons to myself. So care must be taken to allow these things to have an effect on the soul at the proper time.

Among the things that strengthen the control of our I over our astral body, it is important to divert from our souls everything that in any way sets up a contradiction between us and our environment. Of course, it is not among the duties of the anthroposophist to forbid oneself justified criticism. If the criticism is appropriate, then naturally it would be a weakness to pretend that what is bad is good—for purely spiritual scientific reasons, so to speak. But we need not do anything of the kind. Still, we have to learn to distinguish between what we criticize for its own sake and what we find uncomfortable, irritating, because of its influence on our own personality. And the more we can accustom ourselves to make the judgement of our fellow humans independently of the way they stand in relation to ourselves, the better it is for the strengthening of our I in its control over the astral body. It is even good to impose on ourselves a certain renunciation, but not so as to be able to boast to ourselves that we are good people if we don't criticize our neighbors; rather, to make ourselves strong, we should strive not to be distressed by things that we might find distressing only because they are unpleasant to ourselves. And precisely in the area of judging our neighbors, the task would be to apply negative judgements preferably where one doesn't come into the picture oneself in any way. We will soon see that although this looks easy as a theoretical proposition, it is extraordinarily difficult to practice in real life. It is good when, for example, you have been lied to by a person, to hold back your antipathy, the antipathy that comes from his or her having lied to *you*. It is not a question of going to others and further purveying the story that has been told, but simply of holding back the feeling of antipathy from that person having lied to you.

We can certainly use what we notice about people from one day to the next, the way their actions fit together, toward a judgement about them. If people talk one way at one time, and another way at another time, then we need only compare what they do, and we have a very different basis for judging them than if we emphasize their behavior to ourselves. And this is important—that we allow things as such to speak for themselves, or that we understand people as such from their own actions, not judging from individual behaviors but from how their actions fit together. And we will find that even with regard to someone whom we consider thoroughly despicable, thinking, "this person never does anything that would not conform to this concept"—that even with such a person we find a great deal that does not fit in, that contradicts what he or she does. And one need not take into account at all the relationship toward oneself; one can disregard it, and place people before one's soul in terms of their own conduct, if it is necessary to judge them at all. But it strengthens the I if we consider that we could well give up most, perhaps nine-tenths, of the judgements we make. If one experienced only a tenth of the judgements that one makes about the world, really only a tenth, that would be richly sufficient for life. It would not compromise our lives in any way, not even for ourselves, if we decided to forego the remaining nine-tenths of the judgements that we so often make.

It may appear that I have presented trivialities today, but considering such things is our task from time to time. For it can be shown how trivialities can have great effects, and how we must get hold of life by quite other means than we normally do if we are to construct our life in a strong and healthy way. It is not always correct to say, "Well, if people are sick, let them go to the drugstore and there they will find what they need." It would be better for them to order their lives so that they are struck by illness less often, or that sicknesses become less oppressive. And this will be possible if through such trivial things as I have just presented a person strengthens the influence of the I over the astral body, of the astral body over the etheric body, and of the etheric body over the physical body. Self-education, as well as contribution to the education of others, are things that can proceed from our fundamental anthroposophical conviction.

Facing Karma

Vienna, February 8, 1912

AT THE END of the two public lectures I have given in this city, I emphasized that anthroposophy should not be considered a theory or mere science, nor as knowledge in the ordinary sense. It is rather something that grows in our souls from mere knowledge and theory into immediate life, into an elixir of life. In this way, anthroposophy not only provides us with knowledge, but we receive forces that help us in our ordinary lives during physical existence as well as in the total life that we spend during physical existence and the non-physical existence between death and a new birth. The more we experience anthroposophy bringing us strength, support, and life-renewing energies, the more do we understand it.

Upon hearing this, some may ask, "If anthroposophy is to bring us a strengthening of life, why do we have to acquire so much of what appears to be theoretical knowledge? Why are we virtually pestered at our branch meetings with descriptions about the preceding planetary evolutions of our earth? Why do we have to learn about things that took place long ago? Why do we have to acquaint ourselves with the intimate and subtle laws of reincarnation, karma, and so on?"

Some people may believe that they are being offered just another science. This problem, which forces itself upon us, demands that we eliminate all easy and simplistic approaches toward answering it. We must carefully ask ourselves whether, in raising this question, we are not introducing into it some of the easygoing ways of life that manifest when we are reluctant to achieve something in a spiritual way. This is an uncomfortable experience for us and we are forced to wonder whether something of this attitude of discomfort does not find expression in the question that is being asked. As it is, we are led to believe that the highest goal that anthroposophy may offer us can be attained on easier roads than on that taken by us through our own literature.

It is often said, almost nonchalantly, that one has only to know oneself, and all that has to be done in order to be an anthroposophist is to be good. Yes, it is profound wisdom to know that to be a good person is one of the most difficult tasks, and that nothing in life demands more in the way of preparation than the realization of this ideal to be good. The problem of self-knowledge, however, cannot be solved with a quick answer, as many are inclined to believe. Therefore, today we will shed light on some of these questions that have been raised. Then we will see that anthroposophy meets us, even if only by appearance, as a teaching or as a science, and that it also offers in an eminent sense a path toward self-knowledge and what may be called the pilgrimage toward becoming a good person. To accomplish this we must consider from different points of view how anthroposophy can be fruitful in life.

Let us take a specific question that does not concern scientific research, but everyday life—a question known to all of us. How can we find comfort in life when we have to suffer in one way or another, when we fail to find satisfaction in life? In other words, let us ask ourselves how anthroposophy can offer comfort and consolation when it is really needed. Obviously, what can be said here only in general terms must always be applied to a person's own individual case. If one lectures to many people, one can only speak in generalities.

Why do we need comfort, consolation in life? Because we may be sad about a number of events, or because we suffer as a result of pain that afflicts us. It is natural that, at first, a person reacts to pain by rebelling inwardly against it, wondering why there is this pain. "Why am I afflicted by this pain? Why is life not arranged for me in such a way that I don't suffer pain, that I am content?" These questions can be answered satisfactorily only on the basis of true knowledge concerning the nature of human karma, of human destiny. Why do we suffer in the world? We refer here to outer as well as to inner sufferings that arise in our psychic organization and leave us unfulfilled. Why are we met by such experiences that leave us unsatisfied?

In pursuing the laws of karma, we shall discover that the underlying reasons for suffering are similar to what can be described by the following example relating to ordinary life. Let us assume that a boy has lived until his eighteenth year at the expense of his father. Then the father loses all his wealth and goes into bankruptcy. The young man must now learn something worthwhile and make an effort to support himself. As a result, life hits him with pain and privation. It is quite understandable that he does not react sympathetically to the pain that he has to go through.

Let us now turn to the period when he has reached the age of fifty. Since, by the necessity of events, he had to educate himself at an early age, he has become a decent person. He has found a real foothold in life. He realizes why he reacted negatively to pain and suffering when it first hit him, but now he must think differently about it. He must say to himself that the suffering would not have come to him if he had already acquired a sense of maturity, at least to the limited degree that an eighteen year old can attain one. If he had not been afflicted by pain, he would have remained a good-for-nothing. It was the pain that transformed his shortcomings into positive abilities. He must owe it to the pain that he has become a different person in the course of forty years. What was really brought together at that time? His shortcomings and his pain were brought together. His shortcomings actually sought pain in order that his immaturity might be removed by being transformed into maturity.

Even a simple consideration of life between birth and death can lead to this view. If we look at the totality of life, however, and if we face our karma as it has been explained in the lecture two days ago, we will come to the conclusion that all pain that hits us, that all suffering that comes our way, are of such a nature that they are being sought by our shortcomings. By far the greater part of our pain and suffering is sought by imperfections that we have brought over from previous incarnations. Since we have these imperfections, there is a wiser being in us who chooses the road to pain and suffering. It is, indeed, one of the golden rules of life that we all carry in us a wiser being than we ourselves are, a much wiser being. The one to whom we say, "I," in ordinary life is less wise. If it was left to this less wise being in us to make a choice between pain and joy, the path to joy would undoubtedly be chosen. But the wiser being in us who reigns in the depth of our unconscious and remains inaccessible to ordinary consciousness turns our gaze away from easy enjoyment and kindles in us a magic power that seeks the road of pain without our really knowing it. But what is meant by the words: Without really knowing it? They mean that the wiser being in us prevails over the less wise one. This wiser being always acts in such a way that our shortcomings are guided to our pains. We suffer because with every inner and outer suffering we eliminate one of our faults and become transformed into something better.

Little is accomplished if one tries to understand these words theoretically. Much more can be gained when one creates sacred moments in life when one is willing to energetically fill one's soul with the living content of such words. Ordinary life, with all its work, pressure, commotion, and duties provides little chance to do so. In this setting, it is not always possible to silence the less wise being in us. But when we create a sacred moment in life, short as it may be, then we can say, "I will put aside the transitory effects of life; I will view my sufferings in such a way that I feel how the wise being in me has been attracted by them with a magic power. I realize that I have imposed upon myself certain experiences of pain without which I would not have overcome some of my shortcomings." A feeling of blissful wisdom will overcome us that makes us feel that even if the world appears to be filled with suffering, it is, nevertheless, radiating pure wisdom. Such an attitude is one of the fruits of anthroposophy for the benefit of life.

What has been said may, of course, be forgotten; however, if we do not forget it, but practice such thoughts regularly, we will become aware of the fact that we have planted a seed in our soul. What we used to experience as feelings of sadness and attitudes of depression will be transformed into positive attitudes toward life, into strength and energy. Out of these sacred moments in life more harmonious souls and stronger personalities will be born.

We may now move on to another step in our experience. Anthroposophists should try to take this other step only after being comforted many times with regard to suffering in the way just described. What may now be added consists of looking at our joys and at everything that has occurred in life in the way of happiness. If we can face destiny without bias and as though we wanted our sufferings, we will find ourselves confronted by a strange reaction when we look at our joys and happiness. We cannot face them in the same way that we faced our sufferings. It is easy to see how we can find comfort in suffering. Those who do not believe this only have to expose themselves to the experience.

It is difficult, however, to come to terms with joy and happiness. Much as we may accept the attitude that we have wanted our suffering, when we apply the same attitude to joy and happiness, we cannot but feel ashamed of ourselves. A deep feeling of shame will be experienced. The only way to overcome this feeling is to realize that we are not the ones who gave us our joys and happiness through the law of karma. This is the only solution as, otherwise, the feeling of shame becomes so intense that it virtually destroys us in our souls. Relief can only be found by not making the wiser being in us responsible for having driven us toward our joys. It can be felt that one has come to the truth with this thought, because the feeling of shame will disappear. It is a fact that our joy and happiness come to us in life as something that is bestowed upon us, without our participation, by a wise divine guidance, as something we must accept as grace, as something that is to unite us with the universe. Happiness and joy will have such an effect upon us in the sacred moments of our lives and in the intimate hours of our introspection that we will experience them as grace, as grace from the divine powers who want to receive us and who, as it were, embed us in their being.

While our pain and suffering lead us to ourselves and make us more genuinely ourselves, we develop through joy and happiness, provided that we consider them as grace, a feeling that can only be described as being blissfully embedded in the divine forces and powers of the world. Here the only justified attitude toward happiness and joy is one of gratitude. Joy and happiness cannot be understood in the intimacy of our self-knowledge when they are ascribed to karma. If we implicate karma in our thoughts about our joys and happiness, we commit an error that is liable to weaken the spiritual in us. Every thought to the effect that joy and happiness are deserved actually weakens and paralyzes us. This may be difficult to understand because if we admit that our pain is inflicted upon us by our own individuality, we would obviously expect to be our own master also with regard to joy and happiness. But a simple look at life can teach us that joy and happiness have an extinguishing power. Nowhere is this extinguishing effect of joy and happiness better described than in Goethe's *Faust* in the words, "And thus I stagger from desire to pleasure. And in pleasure

I am parched with desire." Simple reflection upon the influence of personal enjoyment shows that inherent in it is something that makes us stagger and blots out our true being.

This is not a sermon against enjoyment, nor is it an invitation to practice self-torture, or to pinch ourselves with red-hot pliers, or the like. If one recognizes a situation in the right way, it does not mean that one should escape from it. No escape, therefore, is suggested, but a tranquil acceptance of joy and happiness whenever they appear. We must develop the inner attitude that we experience them as grace, and the more the better. Thus do we immerse ourselves the more in the divine. Therefore, these words are said not to preach asceticism, but to awaken the right mood toward joy and happiness.

Thinking that joy and happiness have a paralyzing and extinguishing effect, and that therefore a person should flee from them, promotes the idea of false asceticism and self-torture. In this event, we would, in reality, be escaping from the grace that is given to us by the gods. Self-torture practiced by ascetics, monks, and nuns is nothing but a continuous rebellion against the gods. It behooves us to feel pain as something that comes to us through our karma. In joy and happiness, we can feel that the divine is descending to us.

May joy and happiness be a sign of how close the gods have approached us, and may our pain and suffering be a sign of how far removed we are from what we are to become as good human beings. Without this fundamental attitude toward karma we cannot really move ahead in life. In what the world bestows upon us as goodness and beauty, we must conceive the world powers of which it is said in the Bible, "And he looked at the world and he saw that it was good." But inasmuch as we experience pain and suffering, we must recognize what humanity has made of the world during its evolution, which originally was a good world, and what we must contribute toward its betterment by educating ourselves to bear pain with purpose and energy.

What has been described are two ways to confront karma. To a certain extent, our karma consists of suffering and joys. We relate ourselves to our karma with the right attitude when we can consider it as something we really wanted and when we can confront our sufferings and joys with the proper understanding. But a review of karma can be extended further, which we shall do today and tomorrow.

Karma not only shows us what is related to our lives in a joyful and painful manner. But as the result of the working of karma, we meet many people during the course of our lives with whom we only become slightly acquainted, and people with whom we are connected in various ways during long periods of our lives as relatives and friends. We meet people who either cause us pain directly, or as a result of some joint undertaking that runs into obstructions. We meet people who are helpful, or to whom we can be helpful. In short, many relationships are possible. If the effects of karma, as described the day before yesterday, are to become fruitful, then we must accept the fact that the wiser being in us wants certain experiences. This wiser being seeks a person who seems accidentally to cross our paths and also leads us to other people with whom we get engaged in this or that way. What is really guiding this wiser being in us when it wants to meet this or that person?

What is it basing itself on? In answer, we have to say to ourselves that we want to meet a person whom we have met previously. It may not have happened in the last life; it could have happened much earlier. The wiser being in us leads us to this person because of a relationship in a previous life, or because we may have incurred a debt in one way or another. We are led to this person as though by magic.

We now reach a manifold and intricate realm that can be covered only by generalities. The indications here stem from clairvoyant investigation. They can be useful to anybody since they can be applied to many special situations.

A strange observation can be made. We all have experienced or observed how, toward the middle of our lives, the ascending growth-line gradually tilts over to become a descending line, and our youthful energies begin to decline. We move past a climax, and from there we move downward. This point of change is somewhere in our thirties. It is also the time in our lives when we are living most intensively on the physical plane. In this connection, we can fall prey to a delusion. The events from childhood that precede this climax were brought with us into this incarnation. They were, so to speak, drawn out of a previous existence. The forces we have brought along with us from the spiritual world are then placed outside ourselves and used to fashion our lives. These forces are used up when we reach this middle point.

In considering the descending curve of our lives, we perceive the lessons that we have learned in the school of life, that we have accumulated and worked over. They will be taken along into the next incarnation. This is something we carry into the spiritual world; previously, we took something out of it. This is the time when we are fully engaged on the physical plane. We are thoroughly enmeshed with everything that comes to us from the outside world. We have passed our training period; we are fully committed to life and we have to come to terms with it. We are involved with ourselves, but we are primarily occupied with arranging our environment for ourselves, and in finding a proper relationship to the world in which we live. The human capacities that are seeking a relationship to the world are our power of reasoning and that part of our volitional life that is controlled by reason. What is thus active in us is alien to the spiritual world, which withdraws from us and closes up. It is true that in the middle of our lives we are the farthest removed from the reality of the spirit.

Here occult investigation reveals a significant fact. The people whom we meet, and the acquaintances we make in the middle period of our lives curiously enough are the very people with whom we were engaged during the period of early childhood in one of our previous incarnations. It is an established fact that, as a general rule, although not always, we meet in the middle period of our lives, as a result of karmic guidance, the very people who were once our parents. It is unlikely that we meet in early childhood the persons who were once our parents. This happens during the middle of life. This may appear to be strange, but this is the way it is. When we attempt to apply such rules to the experience of life, and when we direct our thoughts accordingly we can learn a great deal. When a person at about the age of thirty establishes a relationship to another, either through the bonds of love or of friendship, or when they get involved in conflict, or in any other experience, we will understand a great deal more about these relationships if we consider hypothetically that the person may have once been related to the other as child and parent.

In reversing this relationship, we discover another remarkable fact. The very people with whom we have been associated in our early childhood, such as parents, sisters and brothers, playmates, and other companions, as a rule are the very people whom we have met in the previous or one of our previous incarnations around our thirtieth year. These people frequently appear as our parents, sisters, or brothers in the present incarnation.

Curious as this may appear to us at first, let us try to apply it to life. Our experience of life becomes enlightened if we look at it in this way. We may, of course, err in our speculation. But, in our solitary hours, if we observe life as filled with meaning, we can gain a great deal. Obviously, we must not arrange karma to our liking; we must not choose the people we like and assume that they may have been our parents. Prejudices must not falsify the real facts. You realize the danger that we are exposed to and the many misconceptions that may creep in. We must educate ourselves to remain open-minded and unbiased.

You may ask what the relation is to the people we meet during the declining curve of our lives. It has been discovered that at the beginning of our lives, we meet people with whom we were acquainted during the middle period of a previous life, while during the middle of our lives, we recognize those with whom we were involved at the beginning of previous existences. But how about the period of our descending life? The answer is that we may be led to people with whom we were involved in a previous life, or to people with whom we may not yet be involved. They will have been connected with us in a previous life if we are meeting under special circumstances that occur at decisive junctures of a life span, as, for example, when a bitter disappointment confronts us with a serious probation. In such a situation, it is likely that we are meeting during the second period of our lives people with whom we were previously connected. Thereby conditions are dislodged, and experiences that were caused in the past can be resolved.

Karma works in many ways, and one cannot force it into definite patterns. But as a general rule, it can be stated that during the second half of our lives we encounter people with whom karmic connections are beginning to be woven but cannot be resolved in one life. Let us assume that we have caused suffering to someone in a previous life. It is easy to assume that the wiser being in us will lead us back to this person in a subsequent life so that we may equalize the harm that we have done. But life conditions do not always allow us to equalize everything, and perhaps only a part of it could be done. Thereby matters are complicated, and it becomes possible that such a remainder of karma may be corrected in the second half of life. Looking at it this way, we can place our connections and communications with other people in the light of this karma.

But there is something else that we can consider in the course of karma. This is what I have called in my two recent public lectures the process of maturing and the acquisition of life experiences. These terms may be used with utter modesty. We may take into account the process by which we become wiser. Our errors may render us wiser and it is really best for us when this happens because during one lifetime we do not often have the opportunity to practice wisdom. For this reason, we retain the lessons that we have learned from our errors as strength for a future life. But what really is this wisdom and the life experience that we can acquire?

Yesterday I referred to the fact that our ideas cannot be taken immediately from one life to another. I pointed to the fact that even a genius like Plato could not carry the ideas of his mind into a new incarnation. We carry with us our volitional and soul powers, but our ideas are given us anew in every life, just as is the faculty of speech. The greater part of our ideas live in speech. Most of our ideas are derived from our faculty to express ourselves in a language. The ideas we conceive during the time between birth and death are always related to this particular earthly existence. This being so, it is true that our ideas will always depend on the where and how of our incarnations, no matter how many we have to live through. Our wealth of ideas is always derived from the outer world and depends on the way karma has placed us into race, family, and speech relationships.

In our ideas and concepts we really know nothing of the world except what is dependent on karma. A great deal is said with this statement. This means that everything we can know in life and acquire in the form of knowledge is something quite personal. We never can transcend the personal level with regard to everything we may acquire in life. We never come quite as far as the wiser being in us, but we always remain with the less wise one. If we believe that we can, by ourselves, know more about our higher self from observations in the outer world, we are being led by our laziness into an unreal world. Thereby we are saying only that we know nothing of our higher self as a result of what we acquire in life.

How can we gain an understanding of our higher self; how do we come to such knowledge? To find an answer, we must ask ourselves the simple question, "What do we really know?" First of all, we know what we have learned from experience. We know this and nothing else. If we want to know ourself and do not realize that we carry in our soul nothing but a mirror of the outer world we may delude ourselves into believing that we can find our higher self by introspection. What we find within, however, is nothing else than what has come in from outside. Laziness of thinking has no place in this quest. So we must inquire about the other worlds into which our higher self is embedded, and thereby learn about the various incarnations of the earth and the world picture described by spiritual science.

Just as we try to understand a child's soul in relation to outer life conditions by examining the child's surroundings, so must we ask what the environment of the higher self is. Spiritual science gives us insight into the worlds in which our higher self lives by its accounts of the evolution of Saturn and all its secrets, of the Moon and Earth evolutions, of reincarnation and karma, of devachan and kamaloka, and so on. This is the only way we can learn about our higher self, about that self that extends beyond the physical plane. If we refuse to accept these secrets we are like a playful a kitten regarding knowledge of our own self. But we do not discover our divine being by indulging and pampering ourselves. Only what is experienced in the outer world is stored inside, but the divine being in us can only be found when we search in our soul for the mirrored world beyond the physical.

The very things that are uncomfortable to learn are the ones that lead to knowledge of self. In reality, true anthroposophy is true knowledge of self. Properly received, the science of the spirit enlightens us about our own self. Where is this self? Is it within our skin? No, it is poured into the entire world, and what is in the world is linked to the self; also, what once was in the world is connected with this self. Only if we get to know the world can we also get to know the self.

Anthroposophical knowledge, although it may appear first as mere theory, points to nothing less than a path to self-knowledge. If we want to find our self by staring into our inner being we may be motivated by the noble desire to be good and unselfish. But in reality, we become more and more selfish. In contrast, the struggle with the great secrets of existence, the attempt to emancipate the higher self from the complacent personal self, the acceptance of the reality of the higher worlds and the knowledge that can be obtained from them, all lead to true self-knowledge.

While contemplating Saturn, Sun, and Moon, we lose ourselves in cosmic thoughts. Thus, a soul thinking in anthroposophy exclaims, "In thy thinking cosmic thoughts are living," and then adds to these words, "Lose thyself in cosmic thoughts."

A soul creating out of anthroposophy says, "In thy feeling cosmic forces are weaving," and adds in the same breath, "Feel thyself through cosmic forces." These universal powers will not reveal themselves when we expect them

to be flattering or when we close our eyes and pledge to be
a good human being. Only when we open our spiritual eye
and perceive how "cosmic forces" work and create, and
when we realize that we are embedded in these forces, will
we have an experience of our own self.

Thus, a soul that draws strength from anthroposophy
will say, "In thy willing cosmic beings are working," and
will quickly add, "Create thyself through beings of will."

The meaning of these words can be realized if self-knowledge is practiced in the right way. If this is done, one recre-
ates oneself out of the cosmic forces.

These thoughts may appear to be dry and abstract, but
they are not mere theory. They have the inherent power of
a seed planted in the earth. It sprouts and grows; life shoots
in all directions, and the plant becomes a tree. Thus it is
with the experiences we receive through the science of the
spirit that we become capable of transforming ourselves.
"Create thyself through beings of will." Thus, anthroposophy becomes an elixir of life. Our view of spirit worlds
opens up, we draw strength from these worlds and once we
can fully absorb them, they will help us to know ourselves
in all our depth. Only when we imbue ourselves with
world knowledge can we take hold of ourselves and gradually move from the less wise being in us, who is split off by
the guardian of the threshold, to the wise being in us. This
wise being, which remains hidden to the weak, can be
gained by the strong through anthroposophy.

"In thy thinking cosmic thoughts are living; Lose thyself in
cosmic thoughts. In thy feeling cosmic forces are weaving;
Feel thyself through cosmic forces. In thy willing cosmic
beings are working; Create thyself through beings of will."

The Four Temperaments

Berlin, March 4, 1909

I T HAS FREQUENTLY been emphasized that human-
ity's greatest riddle is itself. Both natural and spiritual science ultimately try to solve this riddle—the former by
understanding the natural laws that govern our outer
being, the latter by seeking the essence and purpose inherent in our existence. Now as correct as it may be that
humanity's greatest riddle is itself, it must also be emphasized that each individual human being is a riddle, often
even to itself. Every one of us experiences this in encoun-
ters with other people.

Today we shall be dealing not with general riddles, but
rather with those posed to us by every human being in
every encounter, and these are just as important. For how
endlessly varied people are! We need only consider temperament, the subject of today's lecture, in order to realize that
there are as many riddles as there are people. Even within
the basic types known as the temperaments, such variety
exists among people that the very mystery of existence
seems to express itself within these types. Temperament,
that fundamental coloring of the human personality, plays
a role in all manifestations of individuality that are of concern to practical life. We sense something of this basic

mood whenever we encounter another human being. Thus we can only hope that spiritual science will tell us what we need to know about the temperaments.

Our first impression of the temperaments is that they are external, for although they can be said to flow from within, they manifest themselves in everything we can observe from without. However, this does not mean that the human riddle can be solved by means of natural science and observation. Only when we hear what spiritual science has to say can we come closer to understanding these peculiar colorations of the human personality.

Spiritual science tells us first of all that the human being is part of a line of heredity. A person displays the characteristics that were inherited from father, mother, grandparents, and so on. These characteristics are then passed on to the following progeny. The human being thus possesses certain traits by virtue of being part of a succession of generations.

However, this inheritance gives us only one side of human nature. Joined to that is the individuality that is brought out of the spiritual world. This is added to what father, mother, and other ancestors, are able to give. Something that proceeds from life to life, from existence to existence, connects itself with the generational stream. Certain characteristics can be attributed to heredity; on the other hand, as a person develops from childhood on, we can see unfolding out of the center of this being something that must be the fruit of preceding lives, something that could never have been only inherited from ancestors. We come to know the law of reincarnation, of the succession of earthly lives, and this is but a special case of an all-encompassing cosmic law.

An illustration will make this seem less paradoxical. Consider a lifeless mineral, say, a rock crystal. Should the crystal be destroyed, it leaves nothing of its form that could be passed on to other crystals. A new crystal receives nothing of the old one's particular form.[1] When we move on to the world of plants, we notice that a plant cannot develop according to the same laws as the crystal. It can only originate from another, earlier plant. Form is here preserved and passed on.

Moving on to the animal kingdom, we find an evolution of the species taking place. We begin to appreciate why the nineteenth century held the discovery of evolution to be its greatest achievement. In animals, not only does one being proceed from another, but each young animal during the embryo phase recapitulates the earlier phases of its species' evolutionary development. The species itself undergoes an enhancement.

In human beings not only does the species evolve, but so does the individual. What a human being acquires in a lifetime through education and experience is preserved, just as surely as are the evolutionary achievements of an animal's

---

1. Translator's note: The reader may conclude from this remark—for it was, after all, a remark, not a published claim—that Steiner was ignorant of the concept of seed crystals. However, a likelier explanation is that Steiner, whose audience was very likely not a scientifically knowledgeable one, was simply indulging in a bit of rhetorical hyperbole. He doubtless knew that a seed crystal will hasten the crystallization process in a saturated salt solution, but this fact is not really relevant to his point, which comes out only gradually in this paragraph. His point is not that a newly-forming crystal *cannot* receive some contribution from a previously existing one, only that it *need* not; this is in contrast to living things, which require a progenitor.

ancestral line. It will someday be commonplace to trace a person's inner core to a previous existence. The human being will come to be known as the product of an earlier life. The views that stand in the way of this doctrine will be overcome, just as was the scholarly opinion of an earlier century, which held that living organisms could arise from nonliving substances. As recently as three hundred years ago, scholars believed that animals could evolve from river mud, that is, from nonliving matter. Francesco Redi, an Italian scientist, was the first to assert that living things could develop only from other living things.[2] For this he was attacked and came close to suffering the fate of Giordano Bruno.[3] Today, burning people at the stake is no longer fashionable. When someone attempts to teach a new truth, for example, that psychospiritual entities must be traced back to earlier psychospiritual entities, that person won't exactly be burned at the stake, but will probably be dismissed as a fool. But the time will come when the real foolishness will be to believe that the human being lives only once, that there is no enduring entity that unites itself with a person's inherited traits.

Now the important question arises: How can something originating in a completely different world, that must seek a father and a mother, unite itself with physical corporeality? How can it clothe itself in the bodily features that link human beings to a hereditary chain? How does the spiritual-

---

2. Francesco Redi, 1626–1697. Refuted spontaneous generation of living beings out of mud.
3. Giordano Bruno, 1548–1600. Italian philosopher, Dominican monk, burned at the stake as heretic. Taught that the world is infinite in space and time and filled with innumerable suns.

psychic stream, of which a human being forms a part through reincarnation, unite itself with the physical stream of heredity? The answer is that a synthesis must be achieved. When the two streams combine, each imparts something of its own quality to the other. In much the same way that blue and yellow combine to give green, the two streams in the human being combine to yield what is commonly known as temperament. Our inner self and our inherited traits both appear in it. Temperament stands between the things that connect a human being to an ancestral line, and those the human being brings out of earlier incarnations. Temperament strikes a balance between the eternal and the ephemeral. And it does so in such a way that the essential members of the human being, which we have come to know in other contexts, enter into a very specific relationship with one another.

Human beings as we know them in this life are beings of four members. The first, the physical body, they have in common with the mineral world. The first supersensible member, the etheric body, is integrated into the physical and separates from it only at death. There follows as third member the astral body, the bearer of instincts, drives, passions, desires, and of the ever-changing content of sensation and thought. Our highest member places us above all other earthly beings as the bearer of the human ego, which endows us in such a curious and yet undeniable fashion with the power of self-awareness. These four members we have come to know as the essential constituents of a human being.

The way the four members combine is determined by the flowing together of the two streams upon a person's entry into the physical world. In every case, one of the four members achieves predominance over the others, and gives them its own peculiar stamp. Where the bearer of the ego predominates, a choleric temperament results. Where the astral body predominates, we find a sanguine temperament. Where the etheric or life body predominates, we speak of a phlegmatic temperament. And where the physical body predominates, we have to deal with a melancholic temperament. The specific way in which the eternal and the ephemeral combine determines what relationship the four members will enter into with one another.

The way the four members find their expression in the physical body has also frequently been mentioned. The ego expresses itself in the circulation of the blood. For this reason, in the choleric the predominant system is that of the blood. The astral body expresses itself physically in the nervous system; thus in the sanguine, the nervous system holds sway. The etheric body expresses itself in the glandular system; hence the phlegmatic is dominated physically by the glands. The physical body as such expresses itself only in itself; thus the outwardly most important feature in the melancholic is the physical body. This can be observed in all phenomena connected with these temperaments.

In the choleric, the ego and the blood system predominate. Cholerics come across as people who must always have their own way. Their aggressiveness, everything connected with their forcefulness of will, derives from their blood circulation.

In the nervous system and astral body, sensations and feelings constantly fluctuate. Any harmony or order results solely from the restraining influence of the ego. People who do not exercise that influence appear to have no control over their thoughts and sensations. They are totally absorbed by the sensations, pictures, and ideas that ebb and flow within them. Something like this occurs whenever the astral body predominates, as, for example, in the sanguine. Sanguines surrender themselves in a certain sense to the constant and varied flow of images, sensations, and ideas since in them the astral body and nervous system predominate.

The nervous system's activity is restrained only by the circulation of the blood. That this is so becomes clear when we consider what happens when a person lacks blood or is anemic, in other words, when the blood's restraining influence is absent. Mental images fluctuate wildly, often leading to illusions and hallucinations.

A touch of this is present in sanguines. Sanguines are incapable of lingering over an impression. They cannot fix their attention on a particular image nor sustain their interest in an impression. Instead, they rush from experience to experience, from percept to percept. This is especially noticeable in sanguine children, where it can be a source of concern. The sanguine child's interest is easily kindled, a picture will easily impress, but the impression quickly vanishes.

We proceed now to the phlegmatic temperament. We observed that this temperament develops when the etheric or life body, as we call it, which regulates growth and metabolism, is predominant. The result is a sense of inner well-being. The more human beings live in their etheric body, the more they are preoccupied with their own internal processes. They let external events run their course while their attention is directed inward.

In melancholics we have seen that the physical body, the coarsest member of the human organization, becomes master over the others. As a result, melancholics feel they are not master over their body, that they cannot bend it to their will. The physical body, which is intended to be an instrument of the higher members, is itself in control, and frustrates the others. Melancholics experience this as pain, as a feeling of despondency. Pain continually wells up within them because the physical body resists the etheric body's inner sense of well-being, the astral body's liveliness, and the ego's purposeful striving.

The varying combinations of the four members also manifest themselves quite clearly in external appearance. People in whom the ego predominates seek to triumph over all obstacles, to make their presence known. Accordingly their ego stunts the growth of the other members; it withholds from the astral and etheric bodies their due portion. This reveals itself outwardly in a very clear fashion. Johann Gottlieb Fichte, that famous German choleric, was recognizable as such purely externally.[4] His build revealed clearly that the lower essential members had been held back in their growth. Napoleon, another classic example of the choleric, was so short because his ego had held the other members back.[5] Of course, one cannot generalize that all cholerics are short and all sanguines tall. It is a question of proportion. What matters is the relation of size to overall form.

---

4. Johann Gottlieb Fichte, 1762–1814. German Idealist philosopher.
5. Napoleon Bonaparte, 1769–1821. French ruler and emperor 1804–1814 and 1815.

In the sanguine the nervous system and the astral body predominate. The astral body's inner liveliness animates the other members, and makes the external form as mobile as possible. Whereas the choleric has sharply chiseled facial features, the sanguine's are mobile, expressive, changeable. We see the astral body's inner liveliness manifested in every outer detail, for example, in a slender form, a delicate bone structure, or lean muscles. The same thing can be observed in details of behavior. Even a nonclairvoyant can tell from behind whether someone is a choleric or a sanguine; one does not need to be a spiritual scientist for that. If you observe the gait of a choleric, you will notice that a choleric plants each foot so solidly that it would seem to bore down into the ground. By contrast, the sanguine has a light, springy step. Even subtler external traits can be found. The inwardness of the ego, the choleric's self-contained inwardness, expresses itself in eyes that are dark and smoldering. The sanguine, whose ego has not taken such deep root, who is filled with the liveliness of his astral body, tends by contrast to have blue eyes. Many more such distinctive traits of these temperaments could be cited.

The phlegmatic temperament manifests itself in a static, indifferent physiognomy, as well as in plumpness, for fat is due largely to the activity of the etheric body. In all this the phlegmatic's inner sense of comfort is expressed. The gait is loose-jointed and shambling, and the manner timid. Phlegmatics seem somehow to be not entirely in touch with their surroundings.

The melancholic is distinguished by a hanging head, as if the strength necessary to straighten the neck was lacking.

The eyes are dull, not shining like the choleric's; the gait is firm, but in a leaden rather than a resolute sort of way.

Thus you see how significantly spiritual science can contribute to the solution of this riddle. Only when one seeks to encompass reality in its entirety, which includes the spiritual, can knowledge bear practical fruit. Accordingly, only spiritual science can give us knowledge that will benefit the individual and all humankind. In education, very close attention must be paid to the individual temperaments, for it is especially important to be able to guide and direct them as they develop in the child. But the temperaments are also important to our efforts to improve ourselves later in life. We do well to attend to what expresses itself through them if we wish to further our personal development.

The four fundamental types I have outlined here for you naturally never manifest themselves in such pure form. Every human being has one basic temperament, with varying degrees of the other three mixed in. Napoleon, for example, although a choleric, had much of the phlegmatic in him. To truly master life, it is important that we open our souls to what manifests itself as typical. When we consider that the temperaments, each of which represents a mild imbalance, can degenerate into unhealthy extremes, we realize just how important this is.

Yet, without the temperaments the world would be an exceedingly dull place, not only ethically, but also in a higher sense. The temperaments alone make all multiplicity, beauty, and fullness of life possible. Thus in education it would be senseless to want to homogenize or eliminate them, but an effort should be made to direct each into the proper track, for in every temperament there lie two dangers of aberration, one great, one small. One danger for young cholerics is that they will never learn to control their temper as they develop into maturity. That is the small danger. The greater is that they will become foolishly single-minded. For the sanguine the lesser danger is flightiness; the greater is mania, induced by a constant stream of sensations. The small danger for the phlegmatic is apathy; the greater is stupidity, dullness. For the melancholic, insensitivity to anything other than personal pain is the small danger; the greater is insanity.

In light of all this it is clear that to guide the temperaments is one of life's significant tasks. If this task is to be properly carried out, however, one basic principle must be observed, which is always to reckon with what is given, and not with what is not there. For example, if a child has a sanguine temperament, it will not be helped by elders who try to flog interest into the child. The temperament simply will not allow it. Instead of asking what the child lacks, in order that we might beat it in, we must focus on what the child has, and base ourselves on that. And as a rule, there is one thing that will always stimulate the sanguine child's interest. However flighty the child might be, we can always stimulate interest in a particular personality. If we ourselves are that personality, or if we bring the child together with someone who is, the child cannot but develop an interest. Only through the medium of love for a personality can the interest of the sanguine child be awakened. More than children of any other temperament, the sanguine needs someone to admire. Admiration is here a kind of magic word, and we must do everything we can to awaken it.

We must reckon with what we have. We should see to it that the sanguine child is exposed to a variety of things in which a deeper interest is shown. These things should be allowed to speak to the child, to have an effect upon the child. They should then be withdrawn, so that the child's interest in them will intensify; then they may be restored. In other words, we must fashion the sanguine's environment so that it is in keeping with the temperament.

The choleric child is also susceptible of being led in a special way. The key to this child's education is respect and esteem for a natural authority. Instead of winning affection by means of personal qualities, as we try to do with the sanguine child, we should see to it that the child's belief in the teacher's ability remains unshaken. The teacher must demonstrate an understanding of what goes on around the child. Any showing of incompetence should be avoided. The child must persist in the belief that the teacher is competent, or all authority will be lost. The magic potion for the choleric child is respect and esteem for a person's worth, just as for the sanguine child it is love for a personality. Outwardly, the choleric child must be confronted with challenging situations. The choleric must encounter resistance and difficulty, lest life become too easy.

The melancholic child is not easy to lead. With a melancholic, however, a different approach may be applied. For the sanguine child the approach is love for a personality; for the choleric, it is respect and esteem for a teacher's worth. By contrast, the important thing for the melancholic is that the teachers be people who have in a certain sense been tried by life, who act and speak on the basis of past trials. The child must feel that the teacher has known real pain. Let your treatment of life's details be an occasion for the child to appreciate what you have suffered. Sympathy with the destinies of others furthers the melancholic's development. Here, too, one must reckon with what the child has. The melancholic has a firmly rooted capacity for suffering, for discomfort, that cannot be disciplined out. However, it can be redirected. We should expose the child to legitimate external pain and suffering, so that the child learns there are outer things that can engage the capacity for experiencing pain. This is the essential thing. We should not try to divert or amuse the melancholic, for to do so only intensifies the despondency and inner suffering; instead, the melancholic child must be enabled to see that objective occasions for suffering exist in life. Although we must not carry it too far, redirecting the child's suffering to outside objects is what is called for.

The phlegmatic child should not be allowed to grow up alone. Although naturally all children should have playmates, for phlegmatics it is especially important that they have them. Their playmates should have the most varied interests. Phlegmatic children learn by sharing in the interests, the more numerous the better, of others. Their playmates' enthusiasms will overcome their native indifference toward the world. Whereas the important thing for the melancholic is to experience another person's destiny, for the phlegmatic child it is to experience the whole range of a playmate's interests. The phlegmatic is not moved by things as such, but an interest arises when he sees things reflected in others, and these interests are then reflected in the soul of the phlegmatic child. We should bring into the phlegmatic's environment objects and events toward which "phlegm" is an appropriate reaction. Impassivity must be directed toward the right objects, objects toward which one may be phlegmatic.

From the examples of these pedagogical principles, we see how spiritual science can address practical problems. These principles can also be applied to oneself, for purposes of self-improvement. For example, a sanguine gains little by self-reproach. Our minds are in such questions frequently an obstacle. When pitted directly against stronger forces such as the temperaments, they can accomplish little. Indirectly, however, they can accomplish much. Sanguines, for example, can take their sanguinity into account, abandoning self-exhortation as fruitless. The important thing is to display sanguinity under the right circumstances. Experiences suited to a short attention span can be brought about through thoughtful planning. Using thought in this way, even on the smallest scale, will produce the requisite effect.

Persons of a choleric temperament should purposely put themselves in situations where rage is of no use, but rather only makes them look ridiculous. Melancholics should not close their eyes to life's pain, but rather seek it out; through compassion they redirect their suffering outward toward appropriate objects and events. If we are phlegmatics, having no particular interests, then we should occupy ourselves as much as possible with uninteresting things, surround ourselves with numerous sources of tedium, so that we become thoroughly bored. We will then be thoroughly cured of our "phlegm"; we will have gotten it out of our system. Thus does one reckon with what one has, and not with what one does not have.

By filling ourselves with practical wisdom such as this, we learn to solve that basic riddle of life, the other person. It is solved not by postulating abstract ideas and concepts, but by means of pictures. Instead of arbitrarily theorizing, we should seek an immediate understanding of every individual human being. We can do this, however, only by knowing what lies in the depths of the soul. Slowly and gradually, spiritual science illuminates our minds, making us receptive not only to the big picture, but also to subtle details. Spiritual science makes it possible that when two souls meet and one demands love, the other offers it. If something else is demanded, that other thing is given. Through such true, living wisdom do we create the basis for society. This is what we mean when we say we must solve a riddle every moment.

Anthroposophy acts not by means of sermons, exhortations, or catechisms, but by creating a social groundwork upon which human beings can come to know each other. Spiritual science is the ground of life, and love is the blossom and fruit of a life enhanced by it. Thus spiritual science may claim to lay the foundation for the human being's most beautiful goal—a true, genuine love for humankind.

DURING THE LAST TWO DECADES of the nineteenth century the Austrian-born Rudolf Steiner (1861–1925) became a respected and well-published scientific, literary, and philosophical scholar, particularly known for his work on Goethe's scientific writings. After the turn of the century he began to develop his earlier philosophical principles into an approach to methodical research of psychological and spiritual phenomena.

His multifaceted genius has led to innovative and holistic approaches in medicine, science, education (Waldorf schools), special education, philosophy, religion, economics, agriculture (Biodynamic method), architecture, drama, new arts of eurythmy and speech, and other fields. In 1924 he founded the General Anthroposophical Society, which today has branches throughout the world.